BRAND
YOU

About the Authors

John Purkiss studied economics at Cambridge University and has an MBA from INSEAD, where he was awarded the Henry Ford II Prize. He began his career in banking and management consultancy, and has helped to launch several new businesses. John was a Partner with Heidrick & Struggles prior to co-founding Purkiss & Company. In his work as an executive search consultant, John often helps clients and candidates to market themselves. He is the co-author of *How to be Headhunted*.

Further information is at *www.johnpurkiss.com* and at *www.twitter.com/JohnPurkiss*.

David Royston-Lee studied behavioural science at Aston University and occupational psychology at Birkbeck College, London. Having begun his career in recruitment, he became Head of Career Management Services at KPMG. David then worked as Human Resources Director of Ogilvy & Mather. He was Chief Executive of the CAM Foundation prior to founding Partners in Flow. As a business psychologist and executive coach David uses personal brand marketing to help people enhance their careers or change direction.

Further information is at *www.davidroystonlee.com*.

BRAND
YOU

Turn Your Unique Talents into a Winning Formula

JOHN PURKISS & DAVID ROYSTON-LEE

ARTESIAN

Every effort has been made to identify and acknowledge the sources of the material quoted throughout this book. The authors and publishers apologise for any errors or omissions and would be grateful to be notified of any corrections that should appear in any reprint or new edition.

Published by Artesian Publishing LLP
e-mail: info@artpub.co.uk
www.artpub.co.uk

ISBN 978-0-9551164-2-1

Design and Production: Susanne Worsfold

Cover Design: Warren Lambert and Susanne Worsfold

Printed and bound in Great Britain by Bell & Bain Ltd

A CIP catalogue record for this book is available from the British Library.

For Maureen, Alice, Theo and Jemima

"Original insights in a concise format – *Brand You* is an inspiring read."
BB Cooper, composer

"This is a really important book to help you discover your uniqueness and how that contributes to the world."
Nick Williams, author of The Work You Were Born to Do and co-founder of inspired-entrepreneur.com

"Not only does this book set the context for why personal brand building is more important than ever. It also has well-structured, insightful and practical words on what to do about it."
Theresa Wise, SVP Corporate Strategy and Business Development for a global media corporation, Los Angeles

"*BrandYou* is a great book that reflects the age where, to be your best, you need to have a personal brand. If you want to be the first choice on people's list of business contacts, then read *Brand You*."
Peter Cook, author of Sex, Leadership and Rock'n'Roll and Best Practice Creativity.

"People often don't think enough about the impact they have on others, and how they are perceived. This book shows you how to ensure that people's perception of you fits reality. You will have far more impact, which will help you to build a successful career."
Amanda Alexander, Global Head of Talent, Heidrick & Struggles International, Inc.

"A refreshing, insightful and practical guide to managing your most important product – you! Essential reading for anyone who wants to succeed."
Ranjan Singh, Internet entrepreneur, CEO of isango.com

"I was lucky enough to read this book just as I was re-thinking my career. It proved invaluable."
Kevin Mannion, social media consultant

"This is one of the most powerful books I have ever read. Its unique methodology works across all media – it will transform the profile of anyone who reads and applies it."
Kully Dhadda, Director – Flame Public Relations

"*Brand You* is easy to read and absorb. I was able to put the ideas into practice right away." *Naazi Marouf, dentist*

"We find *Brand You* an invaluable tool for helping top-performers become leaders in their sectors."
Frank Lawrenson, Chief Executive, Astror

Contents

Preface

You already have a brand. As Jeff Bezos, the founder of Amazon, once said, "Your brand is what people say about you when you are not in the room". However, most people do little to *build* their brands. They get on with their work, hoping someone will notice them. They may be talented, but they are not well known. They have weak brands that hold them back.

A strong brand will transform your career. This book will show you how to build it. You may object that you are not a brand of soap powder or a soft drink, so the principles of marketing do not apply to you. That is certainly true among your family and close friends. They know and appreciate your many facets. However, other people spend far less time getting to know you. It is best to project a simple message that employers, clients and customers will remember. When they have a need, they will think of you.

We have developed a unique model that anyone can understand and apply. It will give you a deep understanding of who you are and what you do best. These are crucial steps. They will increase your energy and passion for your work – the key to a successful career. You will attract people who want what you have to offer. We will show you how to develop a large, powerful web of relationships that brings you new opportunities and boosts your bank balance.

We strongly encourage you to complete the exercises. *Brand You* is like a guidebook to a distant country. While you are reading about it, you can experience it for yourself.

Acknowledgements

We would like to thank everyone who has contributed ideas, enthusiasm and constructive criticism: Amanda Alexander, Rose Alexander, Mohammad Al-Ubaydi, Dan Andrew, Sue Appleby, Abdul Rahman Azzam, David Badham, Fred Becker, Dr Irina Behnert, Dr James Bellini, Adam Bennett, Andy Black, Martin Bloom, Jo Bowlby, Christian Brensing, Anita Butt, Susan Cayley Pilkington, Chris Charlesworth, Gerry Cheung, Piotr Chmielewski, Semi Cho, Shin Yang Chuang, Charles Cooper, Sara Cooper, Donato Cordeiro, Adam Coxen, Tom Daniel, Shelley Davies, Tony Dowd, Richard Duvall, Dr Barbara Edlmair, Jackie Elton, James Essinger, Jude Flegel, Auriel Folkes, Andy Gannon, Tacis Gavoyannis, Zanna Gayle, Ozana Giusca, Karen Glossop, Shaun Gregory, Nick Grierson, Sanjaya Gunatilake, Julian Ha, David Harding, Caroline Hardwicke, Michael Hartz, Paul Haslam, Graham Hastie, Andy Hayward, Laura Heybrook, Graham Hill, Paul Hinder, Richard Hite, Gary Hughes, Bridget Jackson, Erica Judge, Lydia Kan, Martin Karlsson, Charles Kaye, Bali Kochar, Simon Laffin, Max Landsberg, Shaun Lattin, Frank Lawrenson, Colin Lee, Natalia Leshchenko, Vito Levi D'Ancona, Russell Levinson, Mei Lin, David Lindsay, Bill Lucas, Sarah Lynch, Guy MacPherson-Grant, Eric McClean, Kevin Mannion, Dr Naazi Marouf, Susan Mascarenhas, Martin Mason, Teresa McCrone, Julie Meyer, Andy Milligan, Amanda Morris, Jamie Myatt, Aneta Nawojska, Safaa Nhairy, Janet O'Hehir, Mike O'Shea, Emma Ormond, Denise Parker, Barbara Paterson, Roger Pelliciotti, Anna Persin, Olga Petrovic, Mark Pilkington, Ric Piper, Jessica Pulay, Margaret Purkiss, Simon Purkiss,

Sirish Reddi, Ivna Reic, Mike Richards, Robin Rogers, Daniel Rogoff, Eric Rothbarth, Fraser Runciman, Susanne Rutishauser, Joe Salem, Amanda Salmon, Laura Scaramella, Adam Selly, Harriet Sergeant, Sanjay Shah, Kerstin Shamma'a, Simon Silvester, Isabelle Smail, David Sparling, India Staunton, Andrei Stepanov, Cindy Stern, François Stieger, Valerie Stogdale, Xavier Szebrat, Dr Sándor Takács, Yasuhiko Takayanagi, Ting-Seng Tang, Yin Yin Tang, David Tarsh, Susan Tether, Tim Thimaya, Clifford Thurlow, Max Thurlow, Glenn Timms, Kahéna Tlili, Ted Townsend, Thuy Tran, Elisabeth Tschyrkow, Lawrence Tse, Bhav Ubi-Hull, Mohamed Uddin, Debra van Gene, Andrea von Finckenstein, Amanda Walker, Emily Landis Walker, Ashley Ward, Dave Watkin, Victoria Watson, John Williams, Gordon Willoughby, Charles Wilson, Susanne Worsfold, Clark Zhang and Suzan Ziobro.

We would like to thank and acknowledge those who have taught us, in particular Nella Barkley, Tony Bowley, Professor Ingemar Dierickx, David Fletcher, Sheldon Franklin, Sir John Hall, Barry Harrison, Professor Kevin Kingsland, Julia McCutchen, Barbara Minto, Dr Srikumar Rao, Mike Southon, Dr John Viney and Nick Williams. We would also like to thank Rose Alexander for her advice on legal issues.

1

Why Build Your Brand?

Some people have never seen the need for personal marketing. They do their best at work and are promoted every few years. However, the world has changed.

The typical company man (literally) of the 1950s and 1960s spent his entire career with one or two organisations. Having completed his education and military service, he joined a company and progressed through the ranks. His job title told people what they needed to know about him. In the West this model began to fall apart in the 1970s, when recession led to restructuring and a steep rise in unemployment. From the 1980s onwards, cheap computing power eliminated the need for large numbers of middle managers. Since the early 1990s Eastern Europe and East Asia have embarked on a similar process. In Japan and South Korea, the children of those who worked for one company or the government are changing jobs more frequently. They may even start a business. Another big change is the rising percentage of women in the workforce. In some countries more women than men now qualify each year in law and medicine.

Build your track record

Most of us spend our early years in a hierarchy: in our family, at school, at university and in our first jobs. Some employers offer excellent training and experience. However, the flatter an organisation becomes, the less likely it is to manage your career or keep you over the long term. As a result, you are likely to change jobs more frequently than your parents did. It is better to build your track record than worry about hierarchies and internal politics. If someone fires you, someone else will want to hire you. It is more important to be employable than employed.

With the spread of broadband and mobile communications, we find ourselves in a global market. If face-to-face communication is not required, you can work or do business with almost anyone, anywhere. In the meantime the distinction between employment and self-employment has become blurred. More and more people move back and forth between the two. They train with one firm, join another, lose their job and then move to another sector. They take time out to study or have children. They move to another country and/or start a business. While all these changes are occurring, it is important to stay visible and attract the people who need your services.

Fifty years ago you might have been defined by your employer and your job title. People projected their employer's brand through their dress code, their habits of speech and the way they thought and behaved at work. Hence long-term employees of Procter & Gamble became *proctoids.* IBM, Pepsi and Shell had equally strong cultures. These cultures still exist, but people move in and out of them faster than before.

Instead of pursuing a traditional career, you can now tailor your work to your talents and interests. With less of a hierarchy to climb, you are more likely to move laterally, building your track record as you go. An IT specialist might implement the same software package for various organisations. A director of human resources might help to restructure one company after another. A chief executive might lead a series of companies in the same or related sectors. Each of us develops a combination of skills and experience. The question is no longer simply "What do you do?", but "What *have* you done and for whom?"

Loyalty has declined, commitment is essential
Loyalty is less important than it was. Your employer is not a mother or father who will take care of you in good times and bad. Loyalty is unlikely to be rewarded with job security. Even blue-chip companies fire people who have spent decades working for them. They pay for performance, regardless of your job title. If you build your personal brand, your employer will probably treat you well, in the hope that you will stay. You can move on whenever you want or need to.

While loyalty has declined, commitment remains essential. If you are employed, the best way to keep your job is to do first-class work consistently. The same applies if you are self-employed. If you are known for excellence, clients will keep coming back to you.

Portfolio careers are widespread
Another trend is the growth in portfolio careers, where you combine activities. This is normal in the arts and the media. Leonardo da Vinci combined painting and drawing with designing tanks and helicopters. Comedians

and sportspeople write books. Celebrities appear in TV commercials and play cameo roles in films.

The portfolio approach has spread to other sectors. Some management consultants teach part time at universities. We know a successful investor and company chairman who is also a professional photographer. Some people want autonomy and a flexible lifestyle. Others work on several projects while they look for a new job. Technology has made portfolio careers much easier. Instead of going to the same office every day, you can use broadband and a mobile phone. Women have pursued portfolio careers for centuries, combining childcare with part-time roles. For some this work is now highly paid. Penny Hughes became President of Coca-Cola UK & Ireland at the age of 33. She resigned two years later and has since been a non-executive director of The Body Shop, Next, Vodafone, Reuters, Gap and SEB, the Swedish bank.

One of the UK's best-known portfolio non-executives is Allan Leighton. Since leading the successful turnaround of Asda – alongside the Chairman, Archie Norman – he has been chairman or non-executive director of a wide range of companies, including Royal Mail, Lastminute.com, Bhs, Dyson, BSkyB and Leeds United Football Club. Some companies prefer non-executives who work *full time* in a related field. Someone working in retail might sit on the board of a bank that wants to apply retail disciplines to its branch network.

The number of angel investors has also grown. Some have a full-time job but invest in a start-up company and sit on the board. Others devote most of their time to a portfolio of investments and directorships.

Your network is vital

Your network is an important source of new opportunities. The older you are, the more likely you are to find your next job through personal contacts rather than a recruitment firm. This is even true in sectors with plenty of specialist recruiters, such as finance and accountancy. In the UK, a survey of Chartered Accountants found that networking accounted for 20% of successful job searches for people up to the age of 35. Eighty per cent of them found a job through a recruitment firm. Between the ages of 35 and 50 the ratio was 50:50. For those older than 50, networking accounted for 80% of all successful job searches. If you happen not to be a British accountant, you are even more likely to find your next job through networking, at every stage of your career.

Even if you are busy right now, it is worth keeping an eye on the market for your skills. Your network will help you do this, provided you define what you can offer and what you are looking for. The exercises in this book will help you.

It's not just who you know, it's who knows you

In most occupations lots of people have the skills required. Being good at what you do is not enough. You have to market yourself. If you do first-class work, your boss or client will value you. However, they may still pay you below the market rate. If you make sure other people know what you can do, there will be several of them bidding for your services.

Think of a boss or client who rates you highly. What if you knew ten people like him or her – or a hundred? If more people knew about you, more of them would want to hire you. Your earnings would almost certainly rise. For this to happen, you need to appeal to a much wider audience.

The better you are at marketing yourself, the less you need to sell yourself
Most people probably realise that they need to market themselves. However, marketing does not mean sending out your CV/résumé to all and sundry. That makes you no different from any other job-seeker. As soon as you stop banging on doors, you will be largely forgotten. There is a difference between *marketing* and *selling*. This is how we define them:

- Marketing is building a relationship with your target audience, finding out their needs and telling them how you could meet them. It includes reaching out to new people as well as those you already know.

- Selling is the final stage in the marketing process. It is helping potential customers to make a decision. It is making sure you win a particular contract.

Some people try to sell themselves in the wrong way at the wrong time. You have probably heard them blow their own trumpet at meetings and social events. Both employers and headhunters receive CVs/résumés with long-winded introductions explaining how marvellous the author is. It is a big turn-off. Some people have the opposite problem. They are so terrified of selling themselves that they miss out on exciting opportunities.

The key is knowing *when* to sell yourself. There are times when you are expected to do so. You may be competing for a job or an assignment. It is late in the marketing process and you are already on the shortlist. Your potential employers or clients have invited you to make a presentation. They want to know why they should choose *you*.

How do you get on the shortlist? Other people's perceptions of you play a major role. They also determine the amount people will pay for your services. If you meet someone for the first time, it helps a lot if they have heard or read about you. You already have some credibility on which you can build. Ideally people should experience you in three different ways, in different contexts. For example, they might hear about you, read about you and then meet you in person. They might see you on television or on a well-regarded website. The more widely you are recognised, the greater will be the demand for your services. The most powerful endorsement is when you are recommended to a potential client or boss by someone they trust.

You have been marketing yourself since you were a small child, initiating and developing relationships. The same principles apply in your job or business. Most people prefer to work with those they know and trust. A relationship can last for years – maybe even a lifetime. Every now and then there will be an opportunity to work together.

The best way to market yourself is to build your personal brand
Personal branding is most developed in sectors where the rewards are high. These include the film industry, music and professional sport. Technology and social change have played a major role. During the 1930s Hollywood stars began to become well known outside the USA. There are now hundreds of TV channels, as well as DVDs and

videocassettes. Film stars can now reach a global audience through a variety of media formats. They are marketed worldwide, just like products, services and companies. In the meantime the world's population has more than trebled, from two billion in 1930 to 6.7 billion in 2008.

Musicians and sports people have also benefited. The launch of MTV in 1981 enabled singers such as Madonna and Cyndi Lauper to promote their music through video, while building a strong brand identity. In English professional football, the sale of the UK broadcasting rights to BSkyB pumped money into the Premier League, which became a showcase for players from all over the world. This enabled some footballers to earn very high salaries while endorsing a wide range of products.

Here are some examples of strong personal brands, from a variety of sectors:

Acting:
Jackie Chan, George Clooney, Nicole Kidman, Meryl Streep

Architecture:
Norman Foster, Frank Gehry, I. M. Pei, Richard Rogers

Business:
Richard Branson, Carlos Ghosn, Steve Jobs, Li Ka-Shing

Chefs:
Nigella Lawson, Gordon Ramsay, Marco Pierre White

Classical music:
Thomas Adès, Philip Glass, Arvo Pärt, John Tavener

Fashion:
Georgio Armani, Alexander McQueen, Vivienne Westwood

Fiction:
Paulo Coelho, Milan Kundera, Doris Lessing, Salman Rushdie

Film-making:
Pedro Almodóvar, Ridley Scott, Steven Spielberg

Finance:
Prince Alwaleed Bin Talal, Warren Buffett, George Soros

Motor racing:
Bernie Ecclestone, Lewis Hamilton, Michael Schumacher

Painting:
Lucian Freud, David Hockney, Antoni Tàpies

Photography:
Araki, René Burri, Annie Leibovitz, Don McCullin

Politics:
Angela Merkel, Barack Obama, Nicolas Sarkozy, Margaret Thatcher

Popular music:
Michael Jackson, Paul McCartney, Kylie Minogue

Royalty:
The Queen, Juan Carlos I of Spain, King Bhumipol of Thailand

Sculpture:
Louise Bourgeois, Antony Gormley, Damien Hirst

Sport:
David Beckham, Serena Williams, Tiger Woods

Each has a following, consisting of millions of people. One reason is that the Internet has made them more visible. Some have their own website. There are unofficial ones too, set up by fans or critics. If you want to know about any of these people, you can Google them in seconds.

Other occupations may be less visible to the general public. However, there are strong personal brands in every sector, including advertising, banking, consultancy, insurance, the law, medicine, public relations, consumer goods and manufacturing. Carlos Ghosn, a Brazilian of Lebanese descent, is chief executive of both Nissan and Renault. He built his early reputation in France, where he became known as *le cost killer*. If you type *le cost killer* into Google, there are hundreds of references to him, from all over the world. By any standard, that is a strong personal brand.

Business people deal with brands – their products, services and companies – every day, but often neglect their *personal* brand. However, in recent years top executives' earnings have grown much faster than average, bringing them closer to star performers in sport and the media. Some executives now hire consultants to market them to headhunters and potential employers. There are also public relations firms and advertising agencies that specialise in personal brands.

A brand is an asset in its own right. Agencies such as Interbrand have developed valuation methods which they apply to brands ranging from Nike to Volkswagen. Increasingly brands are being included as assets on companies' balance sheets. Likewise, your personal brand is an asset that can take on a life of its own. If you build it correctly, people will keep thinking and talking about you. Your brand will bring you customers and revenues even when you are not working.

Most of us do not need to be household names. It is enough to be well known among potential customers, clients, colleagues and suppliers, as well as journalists and other commentators who follow our sector. Having defined your target audience, you can work out what you are going to do for them, and how you are going to tell them about it.

The key to building your brand is to know yourself
There are two main approaches to marketing, both of which have their uses. The first is to find out what people want and then develop a product or service that meets their needs. Many successful entrepreneurs are good at this. If their first customer is very demanding, so much the better! Once that customer is happy, the entrepreneur uses him or her as a reference when selling to others. This works with anything from sandwiches to software. It is the 'pull' approach to marketing.

The second approach is to develop a product or service and then find out who wants it. A famous example is the Post-It Note, invented by accident in 3M's laboratories. The company's researchers discovered a glue that could be applied to a sheet of paper but would not stick permanently to anything else. Likewise, when the personal computer was invented, it was not obvious that large numbers of people would want one in their office, let alone at home or while they were travelling. However, the product was marketed effectively and became a worldwide success. This is the 'push' approach to marketing. Something similar happens in advertising agencies. The client has a product or service – which may be new or decades old – and asks the agency to find ways of marketing it. The agency discovers new uses for the product, or variations that make it more attractive to more people.

Personal marketing has more in common with the second approach. The better you know yourself, the better you can market yourself. While you are growing up, you discover you are good at some things and not so good at others. You find some things exciting and others boring. We will start by helping you identify your *talents*. The second step is to discover your *values* – what you believe is important in your life and work. Then you can focus on what you love to do and do well. If you are true to your talents and your values, you will be *authentic*. You will naturally attract people – employers, customers and colleagues – who share some of your values and appreciate what you do best. Whether you are employed or self-employed, they will ask for you.

This does not mean that everyone will love you. Think of your favourite food. Some people love it. Others cannot stand it. The same applies to you. Once you are clear about who you are and what you stand for, some people will flock to you. Others will keep their distance. This makes it easier to find out who wants what you have to offer.

Instead of rushing around in search of your next piece of work, sit back for a while and think about your brand. How you can build it? The stronger your brand becomes, the more easily you will attract the work you want to do – and the rewards that go with it.

2

How Brands Work

Brands in the broadest sense have existed for thousands of years. Empire-builders have long understood their importance. One example is the Lion of St Mark, complete with wings and a book, which was the symbol of imperial Venice. It stands on a column between St Mark's Square and the gondolas. Visitors to Bergamo, far away in the foothills of the Alps near Milan, are sometimes surprised to see the Lion of St Mark on the side of the Palazzo della Ragione. From the fifteenth to the eighteenth century the brand reminded people that they were in the Venetian empire.

Corporate brands have existed for over 400 years. The East India Company was founded in 1600. Since then corporate brands have sprung up in every developed economy. Examples include Benetton, Cadbury, Fosters, Guinness, L'Oréal, Mercedes, Nestlé, Nike, Samsung, Sony and Starbucks. In high-growth economies, alcoholic drinks often lead the way and establish a global presence. Bars and clubs around the world sell Harbin beer from China and Brahma from Brazil, as well as Stolichnaya, the Russian vodka.

The word *brand* has been used in marketing since the mid-nineteenth century, when large factories began to produce soap and other packaged goods. People were used to buying such items from small producers in their local communities. However, the factory owners wanted their customers to trust a non-local product. When the product was ready for shipment, a red-hot iron was used to brand the factory's logo or insignia into the wooden container. Nowadays there are many definitions of a brand. One of our favourites is this: *a brand is a promise kept.* As Andy Milligan, a leading brand consultant, puts it: "a brand is a symbol that guarantees a particular experience."

By marketing a reliable, high-quality product, packaged goods manufacturers attracted millions of customers. Brands such as Kellogg's breakfast cereals gradually became as familiar as local farmers' produce. Manufacturers then learned to incorporate particular *brand values* – intangible characteristics that were important to consumers. Certain packaged foods were homely. They reminded you of the food your mother used to make. Later on they incorporated other brand values such as youthfulness, fun and luxury.

Strong brands have a unique selling proposition and a brand identity

There are two main approaches to brand-building. The first is the *unique selling proposition* – or USP – which is a powerful tool for attracting customers. Not every brand has a single feature that makes it unique. However, you can still have a USP, based on a *unique combination* of benefits to the customer. For example, a cleaning fluid might remove *both* grease *and* limescale. A person could be good at *both* marketing *and* finance.

Some people aim to be the cheapest. However, there are several problems with this. First of all, if you only compete on price you may earn very little. Secondly, any competitor can copy your USP at short notice. All they have to do is drop *their* price. The third problem is that being cheap will drive some customers away. They will interpret cheapness as a sign of poor quality. Top-quality products are sometimes described as reassuringly expensive.

At this point it is worth clearing up two sources of confusion regarding the USP. First of all, we are using the word *unique* in its literal sense. It is derived from the Latin word *unus*, meaning *one*. A product or service cannot be 'very unique'. It is either unique or it is not. Confusion also arises when people talk about 'USPs' in the plural, listing advantages that competitors also offer, such as great customer service and a one-year guarantee. If several people have something, it is clearly not unique to anyone. Your USP can either be one characteristic or a unique combination of characteristics. A clear USP makes your brand stand out in people's minds.

The second approach to brand-building is *brand identity.* One of its strongest advocates was David Ogilvy, the founder of the Ogilvy advertising agency. He argued that brand identity was paramount. In his book *Confessions of an Advertising Man* he stated that advertisers should "build sharply defined personalities for their brand and stick to those personalities year after year. It is the total personality of the brand rather than any trivial product difference which decides its position in the market place."

Brand personalities develop over time, just like human personalities. Some have a heritage stretching back decades or centuries. Several generations from the same family know and love them. You can see this in luxury goods, banking, sports teams, private clubs, charities, cars, cameras, schools and universities. The key is to ensure that the brand identity remains consistent, while the products evolve and the brand itself grows. As we shall see in Chapter 8, *archetypes* are a valuable tool for managing this process.

Some of the most valuable brands have both a USP and a strong brand identity. For example, Coca-Cola has a unique recipe and a brand identity that is known worldwide.

Brands must evolve to meet changing needs
As society evolves, brands must keep up. Attitudes to nutrition and the environment have changed fast, catching some companies off-guard. In the media sector, the switch from print to digital has left some businesses behind. During a period of change, the winners remain true to their *values*: deeply held beliefs which they communicate continuously. Their values enable them to retain existing customers and attract new ones.

In some cases they develop a vocabulary to express what they stand for. Tesco has been very successful at this. Britain's largest food retailer is already in continental Europe and Asia. It is now expanding its chain of Fresh & Easy stores in the USA. Since 1994 its tag line has been *every little helps*. Instead of making extravagant claims which critics can ridicule, it focuses on small, continuous improvements. This slogan has proved highly adaptable. For a long period *every little helps* meant helping the customer save money through low prices. Then more and more people became concerned about wasteful packaging and the need to recycle. Tesco responded by using the same slogan in a new series of advertisements. These showed ordinary people and celebrities transporting their shopping without using plastic bags. A bricklayer carried his groceries on a hod which is normally used for bricks. John McEnroe took a green apple from a tube of tennis balls and began chomping away on it. The phrase *every little helps* has worked consistently during a period of rapid change.

3

Your Brand

As we said earlier, your brand is what people say about you when you are not in the room. What if someone you know was describing you to someone you had never met? What would they say? They might talk about the kind of work you do. For example: "She's a troubleshooter. She turns things around." They might say where you used to work or where you were educated. They might mention your physical appearance, or a sport or hobby that is important to you. If you are related to someone famous, they would probably mention that too.

We will show you how to turn your brand into a valuable asset – perhaps your most valuable asset. As with any other brand, your personal brand is based on people's expectations of how you will behave or perform in particular circumstances. The stronger your track record, the more confidence they will have in you. Your brand is a promise kept. It can be communicated through symbols such as your name, your physical appearance or the way you speak and write. Some people even have their own typeface or logo.

Your brand has two dimensions: reputation and reach

You may have a good *reputation*, but that is not the same thing as your brand. The Latin root of reputation is *reputare* – to think repeatedly. There may be five people who think about you often and ask you to work with them now and then. However, what if fifty or five hundred people kept thinking about you? How much busier and wealthier would you be? The greater the number of people who think about you, the greater is your *reach*. The two dimensions of your brand are shown below:

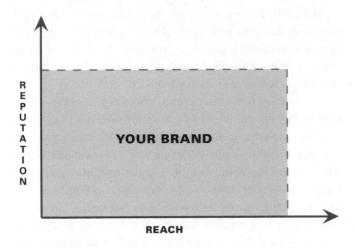

The more often someone thinks of you, and the higher their opinion of you, the stronger your reputation becomes. The larger the number of people who think about you, the greater your reach becomes. In order to build a strong brand, you need *both* reach *and* reputation.

We can all build our brands

Your brand is not static. It is constantly developing. If you are employed, your brand affects your visibility and your job prospects. It also determines the number and quality of job offers you receive from other employers. If you are running a business, your brand will help you win customers and raise money on favourable terms. If you are an investor, your brand will help you attract high-quality opportunities from management teams, advisors and other investors.

Most people have weak brands. When you come back from a conference with a handful of business cards, it is hard to remember who was who, let alone what they did or how you might be able to work with them. As Jonathan Guthrie of the *Financial Times* once said, "Did he import china from Turkey, or turkeys from China?"

If you want to be successful, you must stand out from the crowd. People should remember who you are, what you do, and what makes you different. The stronger your brand, the more people will value you. They will be pleased that *you* are working on their project and may pay extra for that feeling of reassurance. Anyone can build a strong brand, including electricians, disc jockeys, plumbers, cleaners, psychotherapists, lecturers and portrait painters. The professional services sector – including consultants, lawyers and accountants – has grown rapidly. Some professionals spend many years with the same firm, but the issue of personal branding still arises. If you are a junior member of staff, it helps to be well-regarded by several partners, since they will decide who works on each project. They may also support your election to the partnership. Once you become a partner, you suddenly find yourself in a sales role – required to win a certain amount of business. Your personal brand is now more important than ever. Some partners rely heavily on their *firm's* brand, which can help to ensure they are invited to pitch for new projects. However, it is much better to build your *personal* brand, so clients ask specifically for you.

Your brand should be authentic and consistent

A powerful brand has to be *authentic:* based on who you are and what your life and work are all about. You should aim to be the best *you.* Some people project an image that does not fit reality, often by imitating a person they admire or by attempting to conform. The result is artificial and unconvincing. They are sometimes described as *cardboard cut-outs.*

As we said in Chapter 1, the key to building your brand is to know yourself. The first step is to identify the *talents* you were born with. It is best to develop them in a distinctive way, in accordance with your *values.* If you are authentic, people will know what you do and what you stand for. Some people will keep away from you. Others will be attracted to you. If you make it easy for people to see what you do and how you do it, their perception will be aligned with reality. If you then extend your brand into a new area, it will make sense to them. They will feel comfortable working with you in a different situation.

You may wish to keep your work and social lives separate. However, it is essential to be consistent. Some people lead two separate lives which suddenly collide. In one case a young American had been offered a job, subject to satisfactory references. A member of staff at his new company then visited some social networking sites on the Internet. On one of them she discovered his name and photograph, with a detailed description of his sexual preferences. The job offer was duly withdrawn.

The more authentic you are, the more attractive you will be to other people. They will feel they can rely on you to behave in a certain way. Self-employed people often have a natural overlap between their work and social lives. Friends may become customers or colleagues, and vice versa. If so, it is essential to be the same person at work and elsewhere. Your life will then be integrated and harmonious. Instead of wearing different masks, you can be yourself in every situation.

Your brand can become valuable
A strong brand will make you stand out in the eyes of people who want what you have to offer. They will naturally think of you. If your brand appeals to them, they will choose you. They may even pay a premium to work with you. On the other hand, if you do not stand out, they will see you as a *commodity*. Having no particular reason to choose you, they will pay you the going rate at best.

Top musicians and film stars illustrate this principle. Their fans buy *their* latest album or watch *their* latest film because *they* are in it. They earn far more than other musicians or actors. The extra money they earn is only partly due to their singing or acting ability. Film, television and digital media have given them a global market which has boosted their earnings enormously. Personal brands can also acquire an influence that goes way beyond money. Mahatma Gandhi, Nelson Mandela and Mother Teresa have all shaped our world by embodying and promoting a set of *values,* as have Che Guevara, Bob Marley and Mao Zedong.

Some people behave as though they do not have a brand – or if they do, it is worth nothing to them. Some entrepreneurs treat their investors badly when they raise money for a business, assuming they will do so only once. This can make it difficult if not impossible to raise money for a second venture. Other entrepreneurs focus on serving their customers *and* their investors. They develop a following which helps to make their second business even more successful than the first.

Some interview candidates over-promise and under-deliver. They look good on paper. They sound good when you meet them. However, when you investigate their track record, you find they have achieved little for their employers. They often lack authenticity, claiming to have certain values but behaving in an entirely different way. This damages their brand and their job prospects.

Your brand can outlive you
A personal brand can last for decades, even centuries, continuing to sell products and services. Think of Mozart, Elvis Presley, Nina Simone, Albert Camus, Charles Dickens, Jane Austen and Lao Tsu, author of the *Tao Te Ching* over 2500 years ago. William Shakespeare's brand still generates revenues for the Royal Shakespeare Company, the Globe Theatre in London and his home town of Stratford-upon-Avon. Marilyn Monroe died in 1962. Her website – *www.marilynmonroe.com* – offers quotations, news, a fan club and a community section. You can also buy products online.

You do not have to be a celebrity for your brand to outlive you and reach new people. John's father, Ken, was a photographer whose work was published in books and magazines about the countryside. His photos now appeal to a wider market than ever, including a new generation of city-dwellers. See *www.kenpurkiss.com.*

Make sure your name works as a brand

Your name should be memorable and encourage word-of-mouth advertising. More and more of us work in a global market. Can people from other countries remember your name and pronounce it? In some cases a stage name may be the answer. Hence Gordon Sumner became Sting and Paul Hewson became Bono. Madonna Ciccione is known simply as Madonna. Alliteration can also work well, as it has for the artists Gilbert & George.

You may be blessed with an unusual name, but if it is difficult to pronounce, it can hinder word-of-mouth advertising. One solution is to adapt it, as Vincent Van Gogh did when he left the Netherlands to work in Belgium and France. Since he knew his surname would be difficult for foreigners to pronounce, he signed his paintings simply as *Vincent.*

Another approach is to explain the pronunciation in a memorable way. Elisabeth Tschyrkow is an American whose parents were born in Russia. People pronounce her surname in various ways. Some do not even try. The danger is they will remember her as 'the American lady with the unpronounceable name'. Her solution is to write the following on her CV/résumé and elsewhere:

Elisabeth Tschyrkow
(pronounced "Cheer-Co")

Maximilian Thurlow is a young journalist whose full name appears on most documents, including his CV. However, 'Maximilian' is rather long, with lots of syllables. Most people call him Max. From a branding point of view,

Max Thurlow works much better. It is easier to pronounce and remember.

Don't vanish when you change your surname

If you change your surname, it is harder for people to find out what you have done. That may be helpful if you have a criminal record. Otherwise you may wish to keep your achievements visible.

If you are getting married, you can add your spouse's surname to the end of your own. For example, if Susan Bailey marries Fred Walker, she may choose to be Susan Bailey at work and Susan Bailey Walker at social functions. As far as the Internet is concerned, it is better not to place a hyphen between Bailey and Walker. That way, search engines will still pick up 'Susan Bailey', whether she appears in a professional or a social capacity.

You can also set up a personal website that people will find easily if they search for your new or old names on the Web. We will discuss this in Chapter 16.

Your job title is not your brand

Some people aspire to a certain title – such as partner, director or chief executive – and cling to it once they have it. They assume that this is *who they are.* However, your title tells people little or nothing about what you stand for. It does not make you unique. At most, it indicates your position in a hierarchy, and perhaps the skills you possess.

A former colleague of ours has turned around 10 companies, including some large, well-known ones. Although his current title is *chief executive,* he views it purely as a tool to do his job. Sometimes it is an inconvenience. He describes himself as a *turnaround guy,* which is far more meaningful.

Your brand should be like a tall building
Imagine your brand is a building under construction. You want it to be distinctive and clearly visible. Think of the Eiffel Tower, the Empire State Building or the Taj Mahal. As it becomes bigger and taller, more and more people will notice it. They will start to ask what goes on inside. However, before you build it, you must first prepare the ground. This brings us to the subject of your talents.

4

Your Talents

The dictionary provides two definitions of the word *talent*. The first is a natural ability to do something well. The second is a person of exceptional ability. However, the word talent is sometimes used to describe 'anyone we employ and therefore have to manage'. There are even 'talent pools', apparently. We prefer to stick to the dictionary definition. Your brand should be based on your talents – the things you naturally do well.

If your brand is a building, your talents are the bedrock on which it is built. Talents emerge at any time from early childhood onwards. Education can help you discover them. The words *educate* and *education* are derived from a Latin verb meaning *to draw out*. The educator draws out something that is already within you. With training and experience, a talent can be developed into one or more *skills*. Ironically, since our talents come naturally to us, it is easy to neglect them. Some people even focus on their weaknesses instead.

Your talents manifest themselves in what you enjoy most and do best. If you think back to when you really enjoyed your work – and did a great job – you will probably find you were using your talents effectively. You were able to do what was needed and everything fell into place. It may have seemed effortless. People often become immersed and lose track of time. The psychologist Mihaly Csikszentmihalyi describes these optimal experiences as *flow*. You are likely to experience *flow* when you combine your talents in ways you find meaningful, pursuing goals that are attainable while feeling in control of the process and receiving positive feedback. *Flow experiences* help you identify your talents. They also show you the ways of using your talents that you find most fulfilling.

Identifying your talents
The best way to identify your talents is to examine what you have done in the past. Ask people who know you well to help you. They will remember you in different situations. This brings us to our first exercise.

EXERCISE A: Your Talents

(a) Reflect on your life and identify seven occasions that you recall as *high points* or *peak experiences.* (It does not matter how old you were when these high points occurred.) These are memories of times that give you a great sense of pleasure or achievement. They are highly *meaningful* for you. List them in the spaces below. Take them from different areas of your life, including your childhood, education, work and leisure pursuits.

1 ....

2 ....

3 ....

4 ....

5 ....

6 ....

7 ....

If you have more than seven high points, select the seven that stand out for you. Be careful not to select events that you consider socially acceptable or likely to impress others. Choose those that are meaningful for *you.*

(b) For each high point, ask yourself:
   - Which talents was I using the most?
   - *How* was I using them?
   - *Where* was I using them?
   - *Who* was I with when I was using them?

(c) Ask yourself:

- Which talents do I enjoy using the most?
- With what kind of people?
- In what type of situation?

(d) Now list your talents again, starting with those that give you the most energy when you use them:

1 ....

2 ....

3 ....

4 ....

5 ....

6 ....

7 ....

This is an open-ended exercise. As you identify high points, others will emerge. Sometimes those you had forgotten turn out to be particularly significant. It is important to discuss them with people who have known you at different stages of your life. They may remember experiences that you had forgotten.

If *none* of your high points has occurred in your chosen profession or business, it is worth asking yourself if you are working in the right area. High points can provide clues about other ways of applying your talents more enjoyably and profitably. Equally, if all your high points are in the distant past, it is worth asking yourself whether the path you have taken recently is right for you. Maybe there is another that would suit you better.

After doing the exercise, take a moment to reflect. How do you *feel* about where you have come from and where you are going? What are the underlying themes? We will discuss these in later chapters.

We strongly encourage you to complete this exercise, which has helped people in many occupations. Below are two examples: Henry and Elisabeth. Henry is in his early forties. He is British and works in a bank in Geneva. Elisabeth is in her early thirties. She grew up in Hong Kong and works in the UK in sales and marketing.

This is what Henry discovered about himself:

(a) Reflect on your life and identify seven occasions that you recall as *high points* or *peak experiences*.

1. Working on a local farm from the age of seven. This was where I discovered my love of horse riding.
2. Playing football and becoming captain of the school team, while doing fairly badly in my studies.
3. Having scraped into university to study business administration, I suddenly began to enjoy my work and graduated in the top quartile.
4. Taking a year off to work as a volunteer on a project in East Africa.
5. Getting my first job in banking.
6. The successful project that put me on the fast track for promotion.
7. Developing a computer program that transformed how people worked.

(b) and (c)

Based on his seven high points, Henry identified the following talents ranked in order of importance to him:

1. Taking measured risks that raise my level of confidence.
2. Identifying patterns of behaviour among people that cause problems.
3. Identifying people's strengths and weaknesses.
4. Building confidence within teams.
5. Listening carefully and persuading people to take the appropriate action.
6. Examining a complex situation and identifying the simplest solution.

These six talents are based on Henry's peak experiences from the age of seven. Like many of us, Henry has certain talents that he *cannot stop* using. He has a deeply ingrained habit of solving other people's problems. When he looked back over the high points in his life, the theme of solving problems was always there. He loves analysing complex situations and then devising practical solutions.

Here are Elisabeth's high points:

1. Getting the lead role in the school play at the age of seven.

2. Organising a charity fundraising event at school that raised twice as much money as they had the year before.

3. Being elected president of the students' union at university.

4. Winning a place on my new employer's graduate training scheme.

5. A one-year assignment in France, where I learned to speak French.

6. Becoming my company's youngest ever female brand manager.

Based on this exercise, Elisabeth concluded that she had the following talents, ranked in order of importance to her:

1. Strong powers of persuasion.

2. Selling ideas and products.

3. Spotting trends and capitalising on them.

4. Analysing numbers, including financial statements.

5. Adapting quickly to new cultures and ways of working.

Elisabeth has a knack of persuading people to do things and getting them done profitably. Her confidence and persuasiveness, combined with a facility for numbers, have helped her succeed in her career to date.

We hope these examples have encouraged you to do this exercise for yourself. Once you have done so, it will be time to look at your *values*.

5

Your Values

As we said in the previous chapter, if your brand is a building, then your talents are the bedrock on which it rests. Your values are the foundations. Although your values are below the surface, they determine the shape of the building. If you apply your talents in accordance with your values, you can build a very strong brand.

Identify your values

Your values are *what you believe is important.* They are evident in the *way* you do things. Values can range from a belief in hard work or punctuality to deeper principles such as self-reliance, concern for others or harmony with the environment.

Two people with identical talents but dissimilar values are likely to pursue entirely different careers. Imagine two equally talented pianists. One is introspective, deeply religious and shuns the limelight. He becomes an organist in a cathedral. The other is extrovert, loves travel and is excited by the idea of performing in front of large audiences. She becomes a concert pianist. Knowing your values can also help you decide how to apply your talents and build a fulfilling career. You will know which types of work are right for you and which are not. Being true to your values makes you authentic and helps you stand out from the crowd. You become like a magnet, attracting people who hold similar values, whether they are customers, colleagues or suppliers.

The first step is to *identify* your values. The second step is to *project* them. The following exercise will help you.

EXERCISE B: What You Admire in Others*

Write down the names of all the people you admire most, in the space below. Include friends and neighbours, close or distant members of your family, world leaders, authors, artists, sportspeople, media personalities, colleagues and so on. Include the living and the dead. You can also include fictional characters, from television, film or literature. Write down as many as possible – at least 20.

Name

1 ....

2 ....

3 ....

4 ....

5 ....

6 ....

---

* Adapted from Life\Work Design, Crystal Barkley Corporation

7 ....

8 ....

9 ....

10 ....

11 ....

12 ....

13 ....

14 ....

15 ....

16 ....

17 ....

18 ....

19 ....

20 ....

21 ....

22 ....

23 ....

24 ....

25 ....

Now for the second step. Take another look at your list above. Next to each name, write down all the qualities for which you admire this person. Here are some possibilities. We are not suggesting you *should* admire them for any of these attributes. They are just examples: confidence, beauty, persuasiveness, putting their family first, physical fitness, good company, enthusiasm, articulacy, intelligence, honesty, serenity, sincerity, healthy lifestyle, kindness, fighting for what they believe in, hard-working, insightful, loyal to a particular cause, supportive, witty, clarity of thought, sound judgement. We are interested in each person's character or behaviour. If you see the same quality in a number of the people you admire, you should write it down for each of them.

The third step is to review what you have written and think about the qualities you admire in others. Themes will emerge. You will see a number of qualities repeated in slightly different ways. Which of these qualities *resonate* for you? Consider those that appeal to you rationally, emotionally and spiritually. These *qualities* reflect your *values:*

Your values are the qualities you see in the people you admire.

In the space below, write down the five values that matter most to you, starting with the most important:

1 ....

2 ....

3 ....

4 ....

5 ....

When Henry completed this exercise, he produced the following list of people, with the reasons why he admired them:

1. Muhammad Ali – brilliant at what he did. Used his celebrity status for a cause

2. Carl Lewis – a great athlete

3. Bob Geldof – passionate about changing the world

4. Captain Scott – a courageous adventurer who risked everything

5. Ellen MacArthur – determined to succeed

6. My father – amiable, good with people, pragmatic and charming

7. My mother – witty, intelligent, hard-working, resourceful, with strong morals

8. Tim (a friend of mine) – intelligent, kind, thoughtful, great at managing teams

9. Sebastian (another friend) – stoical, thoughtful, energetic, fights for what he believes in

10. Nelson Mandela – courageous. Fought for his beliefs. Suffered but forgave his captors

11. Martin Luther King – a courageous campaigner who died for a cause

12. Steve Redgrave – committed, with the grit to carry on

13. Alex Ferguson – a wonderful appetite for success over a long period

14. Tony Benn – a politician and statesman without ego
15. Peter Cook – a wonderfully innovative comedian
16. Kelly Holmes – overcame injury and persevered to reach her goal
17. Neil Armstrong – a courageous adventurer who risked everything
18. Aung San Suu Kyi – a courageous campaigner who risked everything for her cause
19. Terry Waite – imprisoned while promoting peace and understanding
20. Stuart Rose – visionary, tough, a good manager
21. Richard (my ex-boss) – quiet, gets on with it, brilliant mind, confident
22. George (our former CEO) – engaging, clever, hardworking, strong values
23. Gerald (ex-colleague) – intelligent, strong self-belief, entrepreneurial
24. Helen (ex-boss) – genius, financial wizard, multi-talented, charming
25. Margaret Thatcher – visionary, intelligent, stubborn, insatiable appetite for work

Based on this list, Henry identified the following values, in order of importance to him:

1. Courage
2. Hard work

3. Risk-taking
4. Loyalty
5. Modesty
6. Service to others

He realised that he had been expressing his values through the following activities:

- Working hard to find solutions to complex problems
- Developing new ways of working that are more practical and effective
- Developing his team's strengths through challenging projects

Here is Elisabeth's list of people she admires:

1. Richard Branson – has made money and enjoys himself
2. Bill Gates – has made money. Set up a foundation that supports millions
3. Jill (a friend) – worked her way up from the bottom to become a successful business person
4. John (ex-boss) – intelligent, thoughtful, not motivated by personal wealth
5. My grandmother – worked hard all her life but was always happy and helpful
6. Parents – overcame health problems without complaint and got on with life
7. Frank Lloyd Wright – inspirational architect

8. Le Corbusier – used his talents to devise a new way of living

9. Antonio Gaudí – inspired loyalty to his individualistic point of view

10. Norman Foster – imaginative designs that inspire

11. Frank Gehry – modern art/architecture at its best

12. Francisco Goya – amazing painter. Not afraid to paint what he saw

13. Albrecht Dürer – incredible attention to detail

14. Lucian Freud – shocking, provocative art

15. Kit McMahon – intelligent banker who broke the mould

16. Henry (ex-finance director) – took the time to explain financial modelling to me

17. My maths teacher for his patience and understanding

18. My drama teacher for giving me confidence

19. David Ogilvy – for giving personality to brands

20. Tim (ex-boss) – for having the confidence to let me loose!

21. Jean (friend) – for always being there, always supportive

22. Bob (my husband) – for being a rock. When I am rushing around sorting everyone else out, he looks after me

23. Amy and Scilla (daughters) – for the joy they bring to my life.

From this list Elisabeth identified her top five values:

1. Determination
2. Being positive in the face of difficulty
3. Inspirational leadership
4. Intelligence
5. Innovation

Both Henry and Elisabeth found it very helpful to understand their values. They also mentioned situations where their values had not been respected. This had made them feel uncomfortable, so they had moved on at the earliest opportunity.

Think about organisations where you have worked – and your colleagues at that time. Can you see now why they were right or wrong for you? Think about the work you are doing now. You may feel there is a mismatch between your work and your values. However, maybe the *work* is right for you, but the *situation* is wrong. Some people do well for years in a particular role. Then they move to another organisation where they do badly. Is it them or is it the situation? It frequently turns out that the work is aligned with their talents, just as before. However, there is a clash between their values and the values of the organisation they have joined. If you discover that your values clash with the work itself, it is worth considering any changes you could make. The strongest brands are built by people doing what they love, in a situation that is compatible with their values.

Knowing your values is a great help in building and leading teams. A client of ours is a chief executive who keeps a large white board in his office, with his values written on it. Everyone can see them when they go there for meetings. His values have helped him change the organisation's culture and lead over a thousand people in a new direction. Anyone he interviews can see what he values in other people. They can then decide if they want to work with him.

Now that your values are becoming clearer, it is time to discuss your *unique combination*.

6

Your Unique Combination

You may have one characteristic that makes you different from everyone else. You could be the world's best actuary or the best in the world at selling cheese. However, most of us are not like that. There may be thousands of people with the same professional training as you. However, you have other attributes they lack. What makes you different is your *unique combination* of skills and experience.

A talent can be developed into one or more *skills.* For example, a talent for using words could be developed into the skills of a novelist, a translator, an editor, a screenplay writer, a journalist or a stockbroker – among many other occupations. A talent for spotting numerical patterns could be developed into the skills of a statistician, a code-breaker, an actuary, an accountant or an investment analyst. You could apply a talent for organising people in the role of a chief executive, an army officer or a concert promoter. The more experience you gain of applying your talents in a particular way, the more valuable you become to employers and clients.

To identify your unique combination, you need to understand your abilities and their benefits to other people.

The context is also important. We are looking for the combination that makes you unique *in your environment.* Someone on the other side of the world may have the same combination as you but operate in a different context. Unless you both do all of your business electronically, you will not compete directly.

If asked to describe a friend or colleague, most people would say between two and four things about them. Your unique combination works in the same way. If you state it clearly, it will be easy for people to grasp what you have to offer and then tell others. Many of the best opportunities come through word-of-mouth recommendation. Here are some examples of unique combinations:

- A degree in marketing from the Sorbonne
- 5 years' experience as an account director with Ogilvy
- 2 years as head of strategy at a direct marketing/ digital agency
- Fluent French: written and spoken

- Two-year course in business management
- Qualified lifeguard
- Qualified electrician
- Plays the trumpet in a jazz band

- A degree in mechanical engineering from Imperial College, London
- An MBA from INSEAD
- 10 years' experience in the alternative fuels sector
- 4 years' experience as a business development director

- A degree in communication from Georgetown University
- Five years' experience as a broadcaster and film-maker
- Fluent Arabic

- 20 years' experience in the accountancy profession
- Five years as a non-executive director of public companies
- Experience as chairman of the audit committee of two large companies
- Chairman of an orchestra

Not all the points listed above are to do with work. It may be something else that makes you different. When we run seminars we ask the participants to work in pairs. Each drafts his or her unique combination and presents it to the other, who edits it. This greatly improves the end result. Everything you say about yourself has to be *objective* and *measurable*. The editor rules out vague assertions such as "I am a leader" or "I am entrepreneurial". If you *are* a leader or an entrepreneur, it should be possible to say something measurable, such as:

- Led teams of up to 20 consultants

or

- Founded a retail business whose revenues grew to X million in 5 years

It is best to avoid subjective descriptions such as 'a dynamic person'. Some people may think you are dynamic. Others may disagree. Likewise, saying you are 'a good communicator' does not help much. Few people would say they were bad communicators!

Most people with a few years' work experience have a unique combination consisting of four to six points. You may be unique with only two or three. However, it is best to keep going and consider all your skills and experience. It helps to do this exercise with someone who knows you well, or at least check the results with them afterwards. Having seen you in different situations, they can have useful insights. They may also realise that you have missed out something that you do naturally and take for granted. For example, you may do something purely for enjoyment which might one day become part of your job or business. Examples include photography, music, teaching and writing.

As we said in Chapter 2, you should not market yourself as the cheapest. Anyone can offer to work for even less. Effectively you are telling people that you are a commodity. It is better to base your unique combination on attributes that provide a real benefit to someone. If you build a brand that has significant value for other people, you can charge a higher price while retaining loyal customers.

EXERCISE C: Your Unique Combination

Draft your unique combination, using the spaces below. Think about your education, any skills you have acquired and the industry in which you work. What about the *stage of development* of the organisations where you have worked? Have they been start-ups, turnarounds or companies that were expanding internationally? What have you achieved that is measurable and could be relevant to a new employer or client?

1 ....

2 ....

3 ....

4 ....

5 ....

6 ....

7 ....

8 ....

Here is Henry's unique combination:

- History degree from Oxford University
- 20 years' experience in commercial and investment banking
- Finds simple solutions to complex business problems
- Has boosted efficiency by restructuring divisions
- Strong programme management skills in the application of IT to finance

This is Elisabeth's unique combination:

- Degree in business administration from the University of Hong Kong, where she was President of the Students' Union
- Highly developed sales skills
- Her company's youngest ever female brand manager
- Experience of designing internet sites that increase sales significantly
- A proven ability to revitalise brands that are flagging

People who do this exercise often discover something they have overlooked. They also become much clearer about what they have to offer.

Your unique combination is based on both your talents and your values. It consists of the skills and experience you have acquired by drawing on one or more of your talents. You are likely to have done so in accordance with your values. In terms of the building that represents your brand, your unique combination is the structure that rises from the foundations, before the walls are added. It consists of concrete floors, lift shafts, stair wells, and so on. Your unique combination is built on the foundations (your values) which rest on the bedrock (your talents).

Use your unique combination to market yourself

Once you know your unique combination, you can use it in many ways. For example, you can include it in covering letters, brochures and e-mails that accompany your CV. It will help people to grasp what you have to offer and find ways of working with you. Imagine you are writing speculatively to an employer or recruitment consultant. You do not know their exact needs. However, by summarising what you have to offer, you will make it easier for them to choose you if an opportunity arises. You can write a short letter or e-mail along the following lines:

"I believe I can offer you/your clients the following:

- A 15-year track record in software, including 10 years in sales and marketing
- Experience of leading teams of up to 50 people, based in several countries
- Five years' experience as the chief executive of a high-growth company
- A working knowledge of Mandarin."

You can even use it to extend your activities into new areas that your clients will see as a logical progression. Henry did this at one point. He already had a reputation for solving problems within financial institutions. He then applied his knowledge of computers – that had previously been a hobby – to help a bank process information more efficiently. By combining this knowledge with his financial skills, he strengthened his reputation as a problem-solver.

A lady working in public relations in the metallurgy sector found she was more excited about promoting individuals than companies. She therefore looked for a new role in which she could focus on what she did best. However, it was difficult at first. Her network, including the headhunters she met, saw her as 'a corporate PR executive specialising in metallurgy'.

Your brand often lags way behind what you do now, so it is essential to keep updating people. You may have broadened or deepened your activities, but most of your contacts are probably unaware that you have done so. You can start to expand your business by telling them what you do now. One of the best ways is to give them concrete examples of work you have done recently. We will discuss this in Chapter 11 when we talk about telling your story.

If you include your unique combination in a letter or e-mail, the reader can see at a glance whether you have the skills and experience they need. However, it is also important to know and communicate your *purpose*, which is the subject of our next chapter.

7

Your Purpose

Albert Einstein once said "Strange is our situation here upon Earth. Each of us comes here for a short time, not knowing why, yet somehow seeming to divine a purpose." A sense of purpose helps you focus your efforts, making your life meaningful and enjoyable. You will naturally communicate your purpose to other people, who will understand who you are and what you do. Those who want what you do – in the way that you do it – will be attracted to you.

The diagram below shows how your purpose relates to your aims, goals and plans, as well as specific tasks.

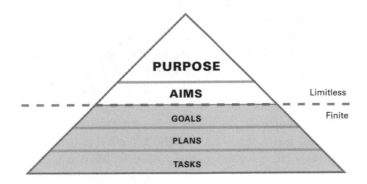

Your purpose ranks above all else. If your aims, goals, plans and tasks are aligned with your purpose, your work will be far more satisfying. For example, your purpose might be to improve people's health. You might therefore aim to cure sick people. Equally, your aim might be to teach people how to stay healthy. You will notice that there is a broken line separating your purpose and your aims from your goals, plans and tasks. This is because your purpose and your aims are limitless. You can pursue them for the rest of your life. There will always be sick people to treat and people you can help by writing books.

Below the solid line are your goals, which are measurable and achievable. For example, you might set yourself the goal of qualifying as a doctor, so you can cure sick people. Equally, you might set yourself the goal of writing a book on a particular aspect of healthy living. Once you have some goals, you can formulate plans to achieve them. Qualifying as a doctor involves a series of tasks, including a course of study and examinations. Some of the tasks will be mundane, such as washing your hands between patients to avoiding spreading germs. However, since this task is aligned with your purpose, it will be meaningful for you. It will help to build your brand.

It is easy to get your purpose, aims and goals mixed up. However, the distinction is crucial. Many people are unaware of their purpose, so they spend their lives pursuing goals. However, goals only stimulate you until you achieve them. Then what? The usual reaction is to set another goal, and another, and another. You may be busy planning and taking action, but the satisfaction from achieving goals in isolation is short lived. It is like being a hamster on a wheel: running hard to achieve a sales target, to save a sum of money or to lose a certain amount of weight. Setting and achieving arbitrary goals does not answer the question *why?* Why are you doing what you do? If you do not know, you may wake up one day and realise that your life is meaningless.

The solution is to look for your purpose. We are not insisting that you define it on paper like a mission statement, though some people find it helpful to do so. Many others find their purpose hard to pin down. However, if you look back over your life and consider the high points, you may identify an underlying *need to do something.* If you ask others how they perceive you, they will often say you have a passion for this or that. They will talk about the things you cannot stop doing. What is the essence of what you do when you are 'firing on all cylinders'? That is when you are pursuing your purpose. If you pursue your purpose, you will be on your way to fulfilling your potential. You will also enjoy the journey.

It helps just to know that you have a purpose. You can use this sense of purpose to make choices that are meaningful and right for you. For example, you might face a decision about a job or business opportunity. Ask yourself "Does this fit my purpose in life? Am I here to do this?" You may get a clear yes or no in reply. If the answer is yes, it is worth investigating the opportunity further. If the answer is no, you can politely decline.

Many people find themselves in the following situation. They have succeeded in one role and are considering what to do next. Then they are presented with an opportunity that uses all of their talents but is very similar to their last job. Do they want to go back to that? Is the role sufficiently energising? Will it fire them up? Is it a challenge they cannot resist, or just more of the same? Do they feel trapped by the suggestion that this is all they can do? If you find yourself in a situation like this, it helps to pay attention to how you *feel*. Does the opportunity resonate with you? Does it feel right for you, or are you simply scared of looking beyond it?

We never tell people that a particular job or business is right for them. Only they can know. Sometimes it is better to leave the question unanswered, at least for a while. As Lao Tsu said, "To know that you do not know is the best". The answer is most likely to come to you when you are relaxed and thinking about nothing in particular. You could be lying in the bath or going for a walk in the countryside. It helps to be away from crowds, buildings and traffic. Some people use meditation to empty their minds of thoughts and emotions. The way forward suddenly becomes clear. It may be a feeling about what you should do next. Some people describe it as an inner voice, telling them which way to go.

Many people find their sense of purpose becomes clearer over time, as they learn more about themselves. By trying different activities you can identify themes that resonate for you. Even an unsuitable job or business can be valuable. It shows you what you *do not* enjoy or do well.

Your aims should emerge from your purpose

Once you have a sense of purpose, you can choose one or more aims that are aligned with it. As we mentioned earlier, aims differ from goals in that aims are limitless. For example, one of the aims of the 'turnaround guy' we mentioned in Chapter 3 is to rescue businesses and help them succeed. He cannot resist reviving a business in distress. This is based on his underlying values, which include hard work, never giving up and acting with a strong social conscience. The talents he applies include analysis, planning, negotiating and persuading people to take action.

Once you know your purpose, you will find pursuing your aims both meaningful and deeply fulfilling. Some people have a clear *calling* or *vocation,* at least for one stage in their life. Doctors are an obvious example. Many of them discover at school that they are good at science subjects and are fascinated by the idea of helping people. The practice of medicine is a way of applying their talents in accordance with their values. However, curing people is still only an aim that reflects their purpose. Many doctors have gone on to pursue other aims that reflect the same purpose. For example, Deepak Chopra is an endocrinologist who no longer treats patients individually. He has written dozens of books on medical and spiritual topics, and speaks to audiences all over the world. Like a number of other doctors, Albert Schweitzer was also a gifted musician. He used the proceeds from his recitals of Bach's organ works to finance a hospital in French Equatorial Africa. He wrote several books and was awarded the Nobel Peace Prize. Top athletes have a sense of vocation that enables them to train hard for years in pursuit of their aims, such as being the best at what they do. However, once they retire it is important for them to find other aims that reflect their purpose. For example, Lawrence Dallaglio, the former England rugby captain, now runs his own corporate hospitality business.

People with a clear sense of purpose usually find several ways to express it. Many of them never retire. They continue to pursue their purpose, moving from one form of expression to another. Doing what they love gives them energy. They may even say they are *putting their heart and soul* into their work. Once you identify and pursue your purpose, it pervades your life. Other people see it in you, in a variety of contexts. You might have a series of jobs or do several related things at once. Here are some examples:

- John's purpose has to do with *transformation*. As a search consultant he helps clients to transform their businesses. Occasionally he also invests in them. His books are aimed at helping people to transform themselves and the organisations where they work.

- David's purpose is reflected in his enthusiasm for developing people. He works with individuals, groups and organisations during periods of rapid change. David helps people to manage their careers. He trains them in groups and leads exercises for teams including boards of directors.

- One of David's clients is an IT consultant whose purpose involves solving problems. She is happiest when solving a difficult problem in a complex organisation. Her purpose also comes across in her leisure pursuits – she is an accomplished bridge player.

Once you have clarified your aims, you are ready to set some *goals.* One of David's goals was to write a book that would help to develop people he had either met briefly or might never meet. One day he took part in a treasure hunt and was paired up with John, who had written other books and suggested they write this one together. The book you are reading fulfils one of David's goals, as well as one of John's.

Your brand should communicate your purpose

If you see a building for the first time, you may wonder what it is *for*. Is it a hospital, a fire station or an art gallery? If it is an office building, what do they actually *do* in there? The same principle applies to personal brands. Small children have been known to point at an adult and ask, "What is he for?" Maybe your colleagues ask themselves the same question about you.

The exterior of a building usually provides some clues to its purpose. There may be a logo that you recognise – perhaps even a slogan. The colour and texture of the surfaces can give you a feel for what goes on inside. Once you enter the building, the ground floor usually tells you a lot more. The people on reception dress and speak in a certain way. There may be a logo with a mission statement and perhaps some brochures or a television screen explaining what the organisation does. You can also get a feel for the culture from the furniture and any exhibits, paintings or sculptures. There may be rock music from an advertising campaign or soothing classical music to keep everyone calm while they wait for their appointment.

Happiness and money are by-products of pursuing your purpose

Richard Branson, the founder of the Virgin empire, once said: "I never went into business to make money – but I have found that, if I have fun, the money will come". In other words, money is not a purpose in itself. If you pursue your purpose then money is a by-product of what you do and the way you do it.

Think of people you know who are highly successful. Our experience is that most of them love what they do. Whether or not they express it in those terms, they exude energy in their work and when they talk about it. Warren Buffett, the world's most successful investor, said "Money is a by-product of doing something I like doing extremely well... I enjoy the process far more than the proceeds, although I have learned to live with those also."

Some people think they *should* be passionate about their work. However, it remains an intellectual idea rather than a feeling. Both of us have interviewed people who said they were passionate but had zero enthusiasm. If you are honest about how you feel, it is easier to identify your purpose.

If you run a business purely to make money, your staff and customers will probably realise and find you unattractive. However, some of them *will* be attracted if you have a strong sense of purpose and love what you do. This will inevitably bring you more money.

Here is an exercise to help you set aside the question of money and identify your purpose. All you need is a pen and some blank sheets of paper.

---

* Adapted from Life\Work Design, Crystal Barkley Corporation

EXERCISE D: A Thousand Times Your Income*

We have some news for you. A distant relative, who you have never even heard of, has died and left you a thousand times the amount of money you normally earn in a year. However, there is one condition: you have to spend *all of it* on yourself. You have *four minutes* to write down exactly how you will spend it.

(Four minutes later) There is a second instalment to the bequest, for the same amount. However, this time you are not allowed to spend any of it on yourself – only on other people. How will you spend it? You have *three minutes* to write it all down.

(Three minutes later) The final clause in the will states that, once you have completed the two steps described above, you will be given unlimited money forever and be granted eternal life. Now that you have unlimited time and money, what will you do? You have *two minutes* to write it down. Please note that your friends and relatives remain mortal.

Now go back and read what you have written. What does it say about you? What is stopping you from doing what you want to do *now?* Are you using money as an excuse for not doing it? What could you do differently from now on? Is there a way of doing what you want without vast amounts of money?

Look at the results of this exercise compared to what you wrote about talents on pages 29 and 30, and about values on pages 36–38. What are the links between these exercises? There are usually common themes. Are there any clues to your purpose? What is the *essence* of the work you do best? What do you do? How do you do it? What is the *context* in which you do it?

This is what Henry and Elisabeth wrote:

A distant relative has left you a thousand times the amount of money you normally earn in a year. You have to spend *all of it* on yourself.

Henry found this exercise difficult. Eventually he wrote the following:

- Learn to fly. Buy a Spitfire for fun and a Learjet 31 for travelling the world
- A Honda Fireblade motorcycle
- An old house by the sea with a paddock and a horse or two as well as a house/horse keeper
- Art nouveau furniture
- A private box at Chelsea Football Club
- Holidays around the world, going to all the places I have ever wanted to visit
- Intensive music lessons on the banjo and the guitar
- Scuba diving equipment and lessons

Elisabeth found it much easier. Her list included:

- A personal shopper for a week's indulgence in London and Paris
- The latest mobile phone and Apple Mac computer
- An apartment in the centre of London
- Tickets to any theatre/ballet/opera I want to go to
- Singing lessons
- Dance lessons
- A holiday walking to the North Pole

- Another holiday in Mauritius to recover!
- A trip to Sotheby's to buy some jewellery and paintings
- A small château in France
- Some intensive French lessons to become fluent
- Some modern art
- An interior design course
- Possibly a course in psychodrama

This time you must spend all of the money on other people.

They both found this much easier. Here is Henry's list:

- Set up a children's hospice
- Set up a fund to give young homeless people a more positive future
- Give to other charities that help people to learn and apply useful skills such as computing
- Make my parents' home easier for them to live in as they get older
- Give all my relations whatever they need most
- Help fund children's sports in my area
- See what has happened to the project I worked on in East Africa and give them something they need for the future

Elisabeth's thoughts were:

- Give money to my husband to develop his business as he wants
- Buy new bikes for the girls

- Air tickets for the family to visit relations in Australia
- Get a full-time carer to help my mother look after my father, who has senile dementia
- Build an extension to my parents' house so we can look after dad better
- Invest money for the hospice I have supported all my life, to pay for extra counselling for the families and more nursing staff
- Set up drama courses in my area for young people
- Give money to Oxfam and Greenpeace

You have been granted eternal life and unlimited money. What will you do? Your friends and relatives remain mortal.

Initially Henry found it difficult to consider eternal life without the people he loved. However, David explained it was an important exercise to help him forget goals and identify his purpose. Henry understood, and then wrote the following:

- Do more to find a partner for the first lifetime
- Consider becoming an expert in some form of conservation – possibly water
- Keep abreast of developments that might affect the human race and its survival
- Ride a lot and become a champion in dressage
- Decide every 50 years which new subject I can excel in and where in the world I will be based
- Become an expert guitar and banjo player

Elisabeth was also not sure she wanted eternal life. It was bad enough seeing her father degenerating slowly. However, she wrote down the following thoughts:

- Work in drama, helping people to express themselves better
- Develop fundraising skills. Work in every aspect of sales, marketing and fundraising, so I can be even more effective
- Set up research into degenerative diseases
- Train in animal husbandry and self-sufficiency so I can advise on and promote it
- Spend time with innovation centres around the world looking for new ways of solving the world's problems.
- Learn to paint
- Become an architect

Is there a way of doing what you want to do now *without* vast quantities of money?

As is often the case, Henry realised that a lot of the things he wanted were within his reach now:

- He could learn to fly. He might not be able to afford a plane of his own, but he could still qualify as a pilot
- He could also buy the motor bike he wanted, second hand
- The old house was too expensive right now but he could rent one in the summer
- He could continue to collect art nouveau furniture gradually

- He could support his favourite football team, Chelsea, without the private box
- He could still visit all the places he wanted to around the world, whenever he had sufficient money and holidays
- Intensive music lessons were eminently possible. He decided to investigate and ended up learning the banjo
- The following year he went to Thailand and went scuba diving for the first time
- Henry found out about a charity that helps young homeless people. He started giving computer training once a fortnight and identified ways to raise money for new computers
- He also got in touch with the project he had helped many years earlier in East Africa and started to investigate how he could help.

Elisabeth also saw that some of her desires were reachable without enormous amounts of money:

- Her husband Bob gave her a day with a personal shopper for her birthday, plus £500 to spend
- The latest mobile phone and Apple Mac were affordable
- Although the apartment in the centre of London was too expensive, she realised that friends who lived there were happy to go with her to the theatre. If she arranged the tickets they would provide the overnight accommodation. This became a monthly occurrence.

- She did not take up singing lessons, but she and Bob started going to ballroom dancing lessons every week
- A holiday walking to the North Pole was possible. After some fitness tests she realised she needed surgery. However, after that she did go for a holiday in Mauritius to recover!
- She did not buy jewellery, paintings or modern art at Sotheby's, but she did go to weekly French lessons

What are the links between these exercises? Are there any clues to your purpose? What is the *essence* of the work you do best? *How* do you do it? What is the *context* in which you do it?

Henry saw several themes in terms of his motivation and relationships. He enjoyed making things run smoothly and helping people to fulfil their potential. Although he did not exactly enjoy public speaking, he realised he could be persuasive and charismatic when he believed in a particular course of action. He was courageous and prepared to take risks when he really believed in something. He knew he could use IT to solve a particular business problem that the software development team had been unable to resolve. They were surprised when he proposed a solution that worked.

However, Henry realised that he did not want to take *physical* risks. Riding a motorbike was more of a dream than something he really wanted to do.

When he really thought about it, the same was true of learning to fly.

As far as he could tell, his purpose had to do with helping people to fulfil their potential and work together harmoniously. This pervaded his professional and charitable work, his horse riding and his relationships.

Elisabeth realised she was more open with people than she had thought, and was not afraid to make a fool of herself. She had no need to be an expert, even though she was in some respects. Her key thoughts related to determination. She was good at getting what she wanted. The more difficult the task, the more she would go for it. What she enjoyed was the challenge of winning. The salary and bonuses were very important to her in terms of visible reward for her effort. In the longer term she saw herself as a chief executive.

Completing these exercises made Henry and Elisabeth's priorities much clearer to them. Henry realised that he had been looking for the wrong kind of partner in his personal life. Above all, he needed someone who shared his values, so he could build a harmonious relationship. Elisabeth realised that she liked being the centre of attention, building something that would last. She also enjoyed looking after other people in a constructive way. Building something for the future came up as a theme in everything she did, from relationships to business.

Some people love what they do and carry on working long after they have enough money to last a lifetime. Pablo Picasso once said that when he worked, he relaxed. Doing nothing made him tired.

Your purpose can be expressed in many ways

Pursuing your purpose could mean you follow a recognised career path. Equally, you might do things that make a lot more sense to you than they do to other people – at least for the time being. George Orwell, the author and essayist, experienced many facets of life that enriched his writing. Following his education at Eton College, he worked in Burma, lived among the homeless, worked at the BBC in London and fought in the Spanish Civil War. These influences are evident in his writing, including *Down and Out in Paris and London, Animal Farm* and *Nineteen Eighty-Four*.

Paul Whitehouse, the comedy scriptwriter and actor, has done a wide range of jobs, including stacking shelves in supermarkets. As a result he writes and performs material that everyone can relate to, regardless of their background. He draws sharp contrasts between different social groups and the way they behave.

Some successful career moves are the result of an accident or illness. One example is Jonathan Shaw, whose young son developed eczema followed by a nut and egg allergy. Realising that other parents of allergic children needed help to find the right products and services, Jonathan launched The Allergy Show, an exhibition which now takes place annually.

Understanding your purpose will help you choose opportunities that are right for you, and politely decline the rest. It can also give you more energy for the things you love to do. You may have a feeling that you are *on the right track*. If you do something new that is aligned with your purpose, you may also experience *beginner's luck*.

We know a hedge fund manager who was offered a very lucrative role in New York. He turned it down in favour of a twelve-week cookery course that he had dreamed of doing for some time. This led him to realise that he needed variety and an outlet for his creativity. He wanted to be entrepreneurial and build up a business, without the need to conform to the structure and processes of a large financial institution. He subsequently joined a smaller hedge fund part time, doing what he enjoys and does well. He is still looking for companies to invest in, particularly those that will fit with his values.

Doing more of the things you cannot stop doing – and which come naturally to you – gives you energy. It also makes life much more enjoyable.

8

Your Brand Identity

We have discussed your talents, values, unique combination and purpose. Our next topic is your *brand identity*, which expresses all of them. It consists of the symbols, signs, language, images and colours that distinguish you from other people in your line of work. This brings us back to what David Ogilvy said about advertisers. They should build "... sharply defined personalities for their brands and stick to those personalities year after year. It is the total personality of the brand rather than any trivial product difference that decides its position in the market place." A distinct, authentic brand identity will help you attract the right employers, clients and colleagues. It will also help them recommend you to others.

Create a distinctive visual style

If you have ever interviewed students for graduate traineeships, you will understand the importance of brand identity. At the end of a full day of interviews, you have met several people in their early twenties. Most of the men have short hair, wear dark suits and are studying similar subjects. It is very difficult to distinguish one from the other. The women have the advantage of variety. You might remember the one with the bright red outfit or the long black hair.

Your appearance is a key part of your brand identity. It is worth devoting time and effort to it. Some people are so distinctive that they are instantly recognisable. Here are some examples:

- Albert Einstein's moustache and wild hairstyle
- Che Guevara's beard and beret
- Margaret Thatcher's hairdo, blue outfit and handbag
- Winston Churchill's bald head, waistcoat and cigar
- Mick Jagger's tongue and lips, that became the logo of the Rolling Stones
- Groucho Marx's handlebar moustache, thick eyebrows and round glasses
- Marilyn Monroe's blonde hair, dark eyebrows and pouting lips

If you wish to be visually memorable, you can also develop or accentuate your appearance in some way.

The way you speak can help to make you distinctive
What do you sound like to other people? There can be a big difference between what *you* hear and what *they* hear when you speak. They hear sound waves travelling through the air. You hear them partly through your skull. As a result, your voice will probably sound harsher to them than it does to you. It is worth recording your voice on high-quality equipment, so you know how you sound.

A regional or national accent can strengthen your brand if there is a positive association with your work. If you are a French-born chef, keeping your accent can emphasise your association with top-quality food. A Californian accent may help if you work in technology. Margaret Thatcher's distinctive voice was a combination of intonation and accent. For Winston Churchill it was intonation and the pace at which he delivered his speeches. Your accent should be *authentic,* unlike some rock musicians whose mid-Atlantic drawl fades minutes into a performance or television interview.

The power of archetypes

Archetypes can give your brand a clear meaning, by communicating *how* you do things. Their origins go back thousands of years, to Hippocrates' *four humours* and Plato's *elemental forms.* The Greek root of the word *archetype* means *first-moulded.* Carl Jung, the Swiss psychologist, defined archetypes as "forms or images of a collective nature which occur practically all over the earth as constituents of myths and at the same time as individual products of unconscious origin."

We recognise archetypes in books, films, products, services and companies. In 2001 Margaret Mark and Carol S. Pearson published *The Hero and the Outlaw – Building Extraordinary Brands Through the Power of Archetypes.* They showed how Jungian archetypes enabled companies to manage the *meaning* of branded products and services. They also suggested that archetypes could be applied to *personal* brands, which is what we will do in this book. Archetypes can be extremely powerful. We have presented this material to audiences of many nationalities. They all recognise the same archetypes.

We can learn a lot from leading actors and musicians. As Mark and Pearson point out, "superstars in the film and entertainment industry, and the agents who manage them, understand that their continued popularity does not hinge simply on the quality or success of the films they make or the visibility they attain. Rather, it depends on creating, nourishing and continuously reinterpreting a unique and compelling identity or 'meaning'." Whatever your line of work, you can use a similar approach.

How archetypes work

Our starting point is that you have a purpose. Developing a powerful brand involves *projecting* your purpose to the outside world. Archetypes can help you do this by representing your purpose in a form that everyone recognises. If your behaviour is consistent with your natural archetype(s), your brand will take on a meaning that increases your appeal to people who want what you have to offer.

Below is a description of the archetypes in Mark and Pearson's model. We have modified the titles and used international examples where possible. As you read the paragraphs below, one may stand out as *your* archetype. Others may fit someone you know. Please note that we do not expect you to fit into a box or *become* any of the archetypes below. Instead, you evoke the archetype in your work. The verb *to evoke* is derived from the Latin verb *evocare*, meaning *to call forth*. When you evoke an archetype, your behaviour and the way you present yourself call it forth in the minds of other people and yourself. We will come back to the question of *how* you do this. In the meantime, here are the archetypes. You may notice that some are prevalent in certain occupations, but not others.

The Caregiver

The Caregiver archetype is altruistic – motivated by a desire to help others and protect them from harm. Personal examples include Mother Teresa, Florence Nightingale and a caring mother or father. Johnson & Johnson, the healthcare company, evokes this archetype, as do private healthcare organisations such as BUPA. Doctors, nurses and social workers often evoke the Caregiver. So do outplacement consultants who help unemployed executives to find a new job. Within a large company, a learning & development director could evoke this archetype.

The Creator

The Creator archetype is often seen in writers, artists, composers, inventors and entrepreneurs. He or she has daydreams and flashes of inspiration which they translate into reality. The Creator is about self-expression, rather than fitting in. When the Creator archetype is active in people, they often feel *compelled* to create or innovate. They have a vision that must take physical form, and they want to create something of lasting value. Examples include Leonardo da Vinci and Wolfgang Amadeus Mozart. More recent Creators include the American artist Georgia O'Keeffe and James Dyson, the entrepreneur and inventor of the bagless vacuum cleaner.

The Explorer

The Explorer – unsurprisingly – wants to explore. Explorers want to maintain independence. They are naturally curious about everything. There is an underlying feeling of dissatisfaction and restlessness. The exploration can be geographical, as it was for Christopher Columbus, Marco Polo and *Star Trek*. However, the joy of discovery can also extend to new products and services. Explorers have an underlying desire to find out what fits with their inner needs and preferences. Richard Branson evokes the Explorer when he travels thousands of miles in a hot air balloon or invests millions in an emerging sector of the economy. Francis Crick and James Watson, the molecular biologists, evoked the Explorer when they discovered the structure of DNA.

The Hero

The Hero acts courageously to improve a situation. He or she is attracted to chaos because it provides an opportunity for heroism. Heroes stand up for what they believe in. There are fictional heroes such as Superman and James Bond. Real-life examples include Nelson Mandela and Aung San Suu Kyi, the Burmese dissident who has spent much of her life under house arrest. Amelia Earhart evoked the Hero when she became the first woman to fly solo across the Atlantic. The police, ambulance drivers and firefighters can also evoke the Hero. Some executives do so when they turn a company around and prevent it from going into liquidation. They may even describe potential disasters in detail to those around them. It adds to the thrill of pulling through and making everything right.

Returning to our example in Chapter 1, here is some online commentary from Tokyo Newsline: "Carlos Ghosn, the ambassador of change, the icebreaker, *le cost killer,* the troubleshooter, or however you wish to refer to him, is Japan's hero. He has provided a glimmer of hope to leaders of thousands of ailing corporations who are desperately seeking solutions to their problems.... Since arriving in Japan, Ghosn has taken Nissan from the brink of bankruptcy to a profit-making entity in just two years."

The Innocent

The Innocent is about fostering purity and goodness. The Latin and Old French root of the word *innocent* means 'no harm'. The primary aim is happiness, perhaps even the experience of paradise. There is a fast-growing brand of smoothie called Innocent. The ingredients are fruit and fruit juice, with no 'weird stuff' – in other words, artificial ingredients. Examples from Hollywood include Tom Hanks in the role of Forrest Gump. Disney evokes the Innocent in films such as Bambi and Snow White. A dietician or someone who helps you stop smoking could also evoke this archetype. Monks, nuns and holy people in many cultures evoke the Innocent. This archetype is also known as the Child.

Some business people evoke the Innocent, at least for a while. One example was Anita Roddick when she founded The Body Shop, which now sells natural skin- and hair-care products in over 50 countries worldwide.

The Jester

On the surface the Jester usually has a good time, enjoying the moment. However, he or she often has something important to say. The Jester gets bored easily and is happy breaking the rules. This archetype can suit consumer brands such as McDonald's, with Ronald McDonald the clown as its emblem. Behind all the fun is a serious business. The Jester has its risks, but has worked well for Ben Cohen and Jerry Greenfield, the founders of the Ben & Jerry's ice cream company. Fun and humour pervade their activities, including their campaign to help combat global warming: "Ben & Jerry's Climate Change College is a launch pad for 18–30 year olds who agree with us that ice caps, just like ice cream, are best kept frozen."

Jesters say things that others dare not say, and can be highly influential. Personal assistants sometimes play this role. Jesters also provoke other people, exposing their prejudices. Sacha Baron Cohen did this as Borat in the film *Cultural Learnings of America for Make Benefit Glorious Nation of Kazakhstan*.

The Lover

The Lover wants to find and give love, and experience sensual pleasure. This archetype is concerned with staying close to the people, surroundings and activities you love. There is an archetypal yearning for true love in many Hollywood stars. It is also seen in products such as perfume, chocolate and ice cream. Fashion models, pop musicians and writers of popular fiction often evoke the Lover.

One of the most famous business people to evoke the Lover is Coco Chanel, who was known both as a dress designer and as the mistress of famous and wealthy men. Sales of her perfume, Chanel No. 5, rocketed once it received the free endorsement of Marilyn Monroe. Chanel had a keen sense of her personal brand. When asked why she did not marry the Duke of Westminster, she replied, "There have been several Duchesses of Westminster. There is only one Chanel."

The Magician

The role of the Magician is to *transform*. One of the underlying themes is discovering the laws of the universe in order to make things happen. The Magician pays attention to hunches and meaningful coincidences. Harry Potter, the star of the eponymous novels, is one example. Another example of this archetype is Paulo Coelho's best-selling fable, *The Alchemist.* The Magician often appears in advertisements for cleaning products, with tag-lines such as "Bang! And the dirt is gone!" A plastic surgeon could evoke the Magician, as could a finance director who specialises in floating companies on the stock market, transforming them from private companies into public ones.

The Ordinary Guy/Girl
Ordinary Guys are OK as they are. They want to fit in and connect with others. Entertainers such as Bruce Springsteen in the USA and Robbie Williams in the UK both evoke this archetype. In the corporate world it is seen in executives who have *the common touch.* Ordinary Guys enjoy self-deprecating humour, demonstrating that they do not take themselves too seriously. They often watch popular sports and have a connection with people that crosses social boundaries. Successful sales people frequently evoke the Ordinary Guy or Girl. When they first make contact with an organisation that could buy their product or service, they chat and build rapport with people at all levels, from the receptionist to the office manager and the boss's personal assistant. This helps every stage of the sales process to go smoothly.

Stelios Haji-Ioannou, the founder of easyJet and many other businesses, illustrates the fact that you *evoke* an archetype rather than *become* it. Despite his wealthy upbringing, he is known for giving the man and woman in the street what they want at an affordable price. Having made his name with his low-cost airline, his subsequent ventures include easyCruise and easyOffice.

The Ruler

The Ruler takes control, creating order out of chaos. Rulers *have* to organise things. Alexander the Great evoked this archetype, as did Margaret Thatcher when she was Britain's Prime Minister. The Ruler wants to create a successful and prosperous family, company or other organisation, but fears being overthrown. SAP, the German software company, evokes the Ruler by helping people who run large organisations to keep things under control. The Ruler is often seen in commercial buildings with Doric columns that recall ancient Greece and the Roman Empire. Rupert Murdoch, the Chairman and CEO of News International, evokes the Ruler as he runs his business empire on four continents.

The Outlaw

The Outlaw is a maverick who rebels and breaks the rules. He or she disrupts the status quo. Outlaw brands include The Rolling Stones, Madonna and Jack Nicholson. Apple Computer also evokes the Outlaw. Its logo of an apple with a bite taken out of it recalls Adam and Eve, who ate the forbidden fruit and were cast out of the Garden of Eden. In the early days this was aligned with Apple's role as the computer manufacturer that challenged the Ruler, namely IBM. Apple remains the preferred option for many 'black-collar' workers such as graphic designers and other creative people. It reinforces the distinction between themselves and the 'suits' who rule the companies where they work.

Entrepreneurs often evoke the Outlaw. They break with convention in order to start something new. One example is Niklas Zennström, co-founder of Kazaa and Skype. At Kazaa he pioneered peer-to-peer file-sharing on the

Internet, resulting in a legal battle with the music industry over breach of copyright. His public profile helped him launch Skype, a service offering free phone calls that became a threat to established telecoms companies.

The Sage

The Sage helps people to understand their world. Plato and Confucius both evoked the Sage. Some universities do so too. They project the message that by studying there you will gain a deeper understanding. Some companies such as McKinsey also embody this archetype, by hiring highly educated people and training them in a particular way. They also publish a journal, *The McKinsey Quarterly*. In a software company, the Head of Software Development sometimes evokes the Sage. If he or she is highly knowledgeable rather than sales-oriented, it is reassuring for both customers and shareholders. Another example of the Sage is Edward de Bono, the author of 62 books including *Lateral Thinking*. The Sage archetype is also known as the Wise Man/Woman.

It is best to focus on one or two archetypes in your work

As we said earlier, none of us fits neatly into a box. During the course of a day you might evoke the Caregiver, the Hero, the Ruler, the Jester, the Creator and the Lover. However, you are likely to be naturally inclined towards one archetype in your work. You will feel attracted to it. People who know you well will recognise it in you.

You will build a much stronger brand if you evoke one archetype – or possibly two – consistently. Consciously or subconsciously, people want to know what you stand for. They also value consistency. If you consistently evoke a particular archetype, they will feel they *know who you are* and can trust you to behave in a certain way. They will feel *safe* around you. They will know what they can ask you to do, if the need arises. All this makes it easier for them to choose you or recommend you to others.

As we mentioned earlier, you *evoke* an archetype rather than become it. Charles is a fund manager who works mainly on his own, with a handful of colleagues, and does not *lead* anyone. However, the archetype he evokes is the Ruler. This is not because *he* is a ruler, but because those who *want to rule* turn to him for help. His ultimate boss has a large fortune that he wishes to protect, along with his family and the country he rules. If Charles wants to keep his job and be well rewarded, it makes sense to ensure that everything he says and does at work is consistent with the Ruler archetype. If he begins to evoke the Jester or the Outlaw, for example, his boss may soon feel uncomfortable.

The Ruler is by no means the only archetype open to fund managers. Some of them evoke the Hero. They take risks and succeed against the odds. Sometimes they produce impressive returns. Occasionally they incur enormous losses. However, investors like Charles's boss have little appetite for heroism. They want to rule their empires and maintain stability.

Life would be simpler if each of us needed to evoke only one archetype consistently at work. However, many people naturally evoke two of them. Here are some examples:

- Henry, who we introduced earlier, evokes both the Ruler and the Caregiver. He helps the bank's top management to keep things under control. At the same time he helps his staff to develop skills that will enable them to progress in their careers.

- The chief executive of a large media company evokes the Ordinary Guy when he builds relationships with his staff, including journalists, sales people, creatives and others from a wide range of backgrounds. He evokes the Magician while he is transforming the company, helping it to succeed in a new environment.

- A business development director employed by another large company evokes the Explorer while she searches for suitable businesses to acquire. She also evokes the Creator when she draws up plans to launch new ventures in-house.

- A doctor evokes the Magician when he prescribes medicine that helps people recover from sudden illnesses. He evokes the Caregiver when he recommends changes in their diet and lifestyle that will protect them from relapses.

- Michael Moore evokes the Jester and the Outlaw. He says things that many people do not want to hear. He gets away with it because he does so with humour.

- Another comedian evokes the Jester and the Ordinary Guy when he makes jokes about himself and his circumstances. People relate to him and his background. They see themselves in him, so they laugh at his predicament – and their own.

- Barack Obama evoked the Ordinary Guy and the Hero when he campaigned to become President of the United States. His campaign successfully emphasised his upbringing in a broken home. The financial crisis helped him to evoke the Hero at a time when voters were already looking for someone who would save them from disaster.

Madonna: a case study in combining two archetypes
Madonna is the highest-earning female singer of all time, having sold over 200 million albums. She was the third of six children born to Italian-American parents. Madonna's father worked in the Chrysler car factory near Detroit. Her mother died when she was six and she was brought up as a Roman Catholic, which has strongly influenced both her music and her imagery. She has both acknowledged and rebelled against her religion throughout her career.

Madonna has followed David Bowie's example by continuously changing her image, thus maintaining people's interest in her. However, in terms of archetypes she has consistently evoked both the Lover and the Outlaw. As she once said, "When I was tiny my grandmother used to beg me not to go with boys, to love Jesus and be a good girl. I grew up with two images of women: the Virgin and the whore." In the 1980s a generation of young women identified with her as someone who fought her way to the top in a man's world while managing to remain rebellious and sexy. By marketing herself as a sex symbol she attracted attention from a male audience at the same time. Some of the key events in her career show how she has built a powerful brand:

- Her strong style enabled her to cross boundaries between audiences. Her music was played in both gay and straight clubs in the United States and appealed to a variety of ethnic groups.
- The launch of MTV, the 24-hour music TV channel, and its imitators, helped her to reach a much larger audience than would have been possible through touring alone. In early 1985 her second album and video *Like A Virgin* made her a fixture on MTV. Video enabled her to control her image carefully and occasionally borrow ideas from Hollywood films, inviting comparison with film stars of the past.
- She recorded other people's songs as well as her own, which helped her to produce high-quality work consistently.
- In 1990, sales of her compilation album *The Immaculate Collection* were boosted by the furore over the video of *Justify My Love*, which was banned by MTV and swiftly became a must-have item. By February 1991 it had become the first video short to sell more than 400,000 copies.
- In the summer of 2006 she became the worldwide face of H&M, the clothing retailer, launching her own fashion line *M by Madonna* in March 2007.

Source: Madonna – *the Complete Guide to Her Music*, by Rikky Rooksby (Omnibus Press, second revised edition 2004)

As far as archetypes are concerned, the main thing is to identify one or two that suit you best – that attract you and make you feel most comfortable. Each of us draws upon other archetypes at various times. It does not matter, provided you are authentic. In other words, you consistently act in accordance with your values.

For example, John usually evokes the Magician in his work. His aim is to help people transform their businesses and their careers. However, when he recruits chief executives, finance directors or non-executive directors he often evokes the Ruler. When he writes books he evokes an element of the Creator. As a consultant, David works with a wide range of organisations. Although he is most comfortable evoking the Magician or the Caregiver, he sometimes needs to evoke the Outlaw or the Jester for a specific reason.

Your archetype(s) may differ from your employer's

You do not have to evoke the same archetype(s) as the organisation where you work. For example, we know an all-day café that evokes the Innocent. The ingredients are pure and fresh. The Italian flat bread is baked on site. However, the founder embodies *both* the Innocent *and* the Creator. While he develops the recipes himself – and safeguards the purity of the brand – this is his third start-up. One day he plans to spend more time on creative writing. It helps that his investors see both the Innocent and the Creator in him. They realise that he is intent on creating a profitable business as well as baking nice bread.

Here is a summary of the archetypes we have discussed in this book:

The Caregiver	Helps and protects from harm
The Creator	Compelled to create and innovate
The Explorer	Explores and discovers
The Hero	Acts courageously to put things right
The Innocent	Seeks purity, goodness and happiness
The Jester	Has a good time but may convey a serious message
The Lover	Finds and gives love and sensual pleasure
The Magician	Transforms situations
The Ordinary Guy/Girl	OK as he or she is. Connects with others
The Ruler	Takes control. Creates order out of chaos
The Outlaw	Rebels and breaks the rules
The Sage	Helps people to understand their world

It is now time to identify *your* archetype(s). The following exercise will help you.

EXERCISE E: Your Archetype(s)

Refer to Exercises B and D, which you completed on pages 36 and 61. Take another look at your top five values and your purpose. Do they suggest an archetype that you evoke naturally? Show the description of the archetypes on pages 75–81 to seven colleagues and/or friends. Include people you have known for a short while. Ask them which archetype(s) they can identify in you. If you and they pick the same archetype(s), then you have a clear brand identity. If they pick a range of different archetypes, it means your brand is not clearly defined.

Henry realised that he evoked both the Ruler and the Caregiver. He is trusted and respected by the bank's top management. They count on him to manage and control projects successfully. It helps them to Rule. At the same time he helps his staff to develop new skills, so they can progress in their careers. He is committed to helping those who need support, thereby evoking the Caregiver. He prefers to work quietly, building his arguments on strong logical foundations, ensuring that the strategy fits the needs of the staff, the management and the shareholders.

Elisabeth was attracted to the Hero archetype above all others. She felt she worked best that way and enjoyed the challenge of doing things better than ever before. If a business was underperforming, she took great pleasure in making rapid improvements. She also evoked the Creator, with her emphasis on building lasting relationships and robust organisations.

You may be tempted to keep your options open by giving different messages to different people. However, by trying to appeal to everyone, you can fail to appeal strongly to *anyone*. Think of washing powder in your local supermarket. Some brands wash whiter than white. Others keep your colours bright. Some are designed to protect people with allergies. Each has a unique appeal. One will stand out as the best for the purpose you have in mind, while others blend into the background. No one wants a washing powder that may perhaps be quite good for something or other.

Many of us face too many choices and have to process too much information. Brands simplify our decisions and give us a feeling of certainty. In most product categories the majority of people can only remember two or three leading brands. In cola beverages, it could be Coke, Pepsi and...?

The same applies to people who are considering using your services. The clearer the image of what you do and what you stand for, the easier it will be for them to choose *you*. Once you have identified the archetype you evoke *naturally*, it is important to do so *consistently* in the eyes of your target market. You should be the first or second person they think of whenever they have a need. Many people want a choice of supplier, but they do not need more than two or three to choose from. Make sure you are one of them!

Your brand identity is like the exterior and interior of a building. They tell people what it is for and how things are done there. When you walk into a bank with Doric columns made of granite, you will probably have a feeling of solidity and security. The building evokes the Ruler, giving the impression that your savings are likely to be safe there. When someone walks into a health food store, they see the nuts, seeds and dried fruit in simple packaging. They notice the stripped pine shelving. The surroundings evoke the Innocent.

9

Focusing on your Purpose

Once you know your main archetype you can seek opportunities to evoke it. This will help you focus on your purpose and avoid being distracted. If your brand is a building then each successful project adds a storey. It will gradually become a landmark.

Jobs, businesses and short-term contracts are *vehicles* for pursuing your purpose. It is important to choose the right vehicle for you. However, some people apply for any job they have the faintest chance of getting. They risk ending up in a role that does not suit them. It is better to steer clear of employers who do not want what you enjoy doing most. You will save everyone a lot of time and trouble. In Chapter 3 we mentioned the chief executive who describes himself as a 'turnaround guy', consistently evoking the Hero. Once his task is complete he leaves the company. Then he looks for the next opportunity to carry out an Heroic rescue.

It takes courage to focus on your purpose and your archetype. However, it is much more rewarding than randomly pestering people for a job. Knowing your purpose makes it easier to spot opportunities that are right for you. It also helps you to ask the right questions and find out if the culture fits your way of working. The clearer you are about what you want, the more likely you are to get it. Your thoughts, feelings and actions will send out a consistent message.

Choose your customers and projects with care
Whether you are employed or self-employed, it is worth considering the effect that each new customer or client will have on your brand. Salespeople are remembered for winning a particular contract that boosted their company or threatened its survival. Bankers, advertising executives, public relations consultants and headhunters are all judged by the clients they represent.

If the work itself fills you with enthusiasm, you are likely to do an excellent job and strengthen your brand. However, some people take on work they find uninspiring, feeling they have to prove themselves. Unfortunately, *you are what you eat.* You will become known for the work you find uninspiring and attract more of the same. You may also discourage people from giving you projects you would find more exciting.

A client of David's is a human resources director who became a self-employed consultant. She planned to focus on highly-paid strategic work. Then someone asked her to deal with a complicated bullying case, which she handled as a favour. This led to more of the same. As word spread that she was the expert in bullying, she attracted more problems and less of the work she wanted to do.

Some people take on lots of projects just to keep their plates full. If you are employed, you may have to do this in order to meet your budget and keep your job. However, if the work does not fit your purpose, it can dilute your focus and weaken your brand. If you decline it, you can spend the time saved on activities that will build your brand and increase your revenues. For example, you could speak at a conference or write an article that potential clients will read.

Turning work down can feel like a brave thing to do. However, once you get used to doing what inspires you, you will feel more confident about it. Your state of mind is just as important as your marketing efforts in attracting the work you really want to do.

Continuously improve what you do

The world moves on and so should you. We can all improve the way we serve people. If you are committed to what you do, and excited about it, you will have the energy you need to keep learning and improving. Your work should be:

1. Top-quality
2. Distinctive
3. Consistent with your values and your purpose
4. Valuable to the people you serve

What about the quality of your work? If you look carefully you can always find ways to do it better. One example is written documents. Some people speak fluently but write carelessly. Their documents are hard to read and understand. Once they begin to circulate, they damage that person's brand. Think of your written work as an advertisement. If it is succinct and clear, it will enhance your reputation for quality. Imagine you are going to read it aloud on national radio. That will help you to produce a first-class document.

It is important to be *distinctive* in ways that are consistent with your values and your purpose. This could include any *pro bono* or voluntary work you do. David Beckham's football academies are one example. Roger Moore, the actor who played James Bond, has worked as a UNICEF Goodwill Ambassador. In our earlier examples Henry used his ability to develop people in his voluntary work with homeless people. Elisabeth applied her sales skills to fundraising for a charity. In both cases their voluntary work was consistent with their values and their purpose.

For your work to be *valuable* to your clients it must meet their needs, some of which may be unspoken. We know a dentist who was one of the first in the UK to offer tooth whitening. He now also offers Botox, based on his knowledge of facial musculature. While few people would walk into a dental surgery looking for that treatment, many have responded to the poster in his waiting room. He knows his patients care about their appearance as well as their health.

If you are a specialist in one area, you can play to your strengths while seizing opportunities in other, related areas. We know a medical doctor who works as a coroner. He has also become a consultant to film directors. He helps them and their special-effects teams to ensure that every illness or injury is true to life.

Ask for feedback
The moment of truth comes when you start working on a project. Some clients and employers will give you feedback as you go along. Others prefer to do so once you have finished. You may be reluctant to ask for feedback, if you are afraid of criticism. However, it becomes much easier if you are committed to being excellent at what you do.

Imagine you are a food manufacturer testing a new recipe on consumers. Some may loathe your latest concoction. However, if you absorb their feedback and adapt your recipe, they will keep buying from you. Even in difficult situations, feedback can *strengthen* your relationship if your client senses your commitment. They will have even more reason to keep working with you, since you have shown you are responsive.

Clients of executive search firms are usually impressed if a headhunter admits to a problem and makes strenuous efforts to resolve it. We are not recommending you deliberately create problems. However, they can be an opportunity to demonstrate your values and your commitment to your purpose. Your clients may surprise you by recommending you to other people.

10

Your Contacts

As the saying goes, *every opportunity begins with a relationship.* When you build your brand you strengthen existing relationships and create new ones. It is best to start with your existing contacts. Imagine you are standing within several overlapping circles. Each circle represents a group of people with whom you have a connection. Maybe you grew up, studied, worked or played sport together. They could be members of your family, your local community or some other group.

The following exercise will help you draw up your list of contacts.

EXERCISE F: Creating Your Contact List
Take a blank sheet of paper, or a spreadsheet such as Excel on your computer. If you use a spreadsheet, you can change the format as your list evolves. We are going to make a list of *all* your contacts, whether or not you believe they can help you. This exercise will help you to think broadly, without pre-judging.

1. In the first two columns, insert the first and second names of your past and present bosses or clients. Be sure to include anyone who is so happy with your service that they recommend you to other people. These people are sometimes described as *evangelists.*

2. Now insert the names of your colleagues, past and present. Make sure you include those who are more senior than you, as well as those who are more junior. Focus on people you respect and would like to stay in touch with.

3. Add the names of your advisors, in both your private and professional life. Include doctors, lawyers, accountants, tax advisors, bankers, estate agents and recruitment consultants, for example.

4. Add the names of all the members of your family.

5. Add the names of all your friends and acquaintances. Start with those closest to you and work outwards. You may feel inclined to exclude people who have nothing to do with your work. However, there are many examples of a friend or relative making a personal introduction that transformed someone's career.

6. Now think of any journalists you know, in the press, on the radio, on television and online.

7. What about people who are significantly younger than you? Many of us overlook these contacts because we are focused on those who are some way ahead of us. Younger people often move in completely different circles. Some may be highly motivated to help you.

8. If you are looking for a job, include potential employers you have already met or spoken to. Even if you do not end up working for them, you may be able to help each other in some other way.

9. Add the names of any potential clients you have met or spoken to.

10. Looking back over the list, make sure you have included any networkers with large address books who habitually put people in touch with each other. In *The Tipping Point,* Malcolm Gladwell describes these people as *Connectors*. They are very effective at spreading the word about you.

Now you have your list, you can add the names of people you meet for the first time – if you get on well with them. Remember that you are building relationships with *people* rather than job titles.

Initially Henry found it difficult to complete the list of contacts, since he kept wondering how he was supposed to use it. However, he then realised that he knew a lot of people and wrote down everyone he could think of.

Elisabeth already had a list of 370 people with whom she stayed in regular contact. Some were connected to her on the Internet, on LinkedIn. She had already used her network to find her present job and did her best to contact certain people at least once a quarter.

You could of course ignore this exercise and contact people you have never met. That might work if you approached enough of them. However, given a choice, most of us prefer to work with those we know and trust. If you only contact strangers, you will have to build each relationship from scratch. The advantage of starting with your existing contacts is that many of them feel comfortable with you already. Some will recommend you to others, so you build new relationships faster. Your relationships should survive the moves that either of you makes from one organisation to another.

If you are reluctant to contact the people you know, there may be a clash between your work and your values. If you believe in what you are doing, then the people you know are the obvious starting point.

As we said in Chapter 1, "marketing is building a relationship with your target audience, finding out their needs and telling them how you could meet them. It includes reaching out to new people as well as those you already know." Your list makes it easy to keep track of when you have contacted people, on a variety of subjects. It could look like this:

First Name	Surname	E-mail about XYZ	Attended our event at ABC	Our booklet about ...	Christmas/ birthday card
Peter	Brown	5/5/2012	7/7/2012	5/8/2012	
Mike	Green	8/6/2012	7/7/2012	9/8/2012	
Jane	Smith	4/6/2012	7/7/2012	6/8/2012	

Whenever you contact someone on your list, insert a date in the appropriate column. If you are looking for a job, you can use the list to keep track of interviews and follow up efficiently. You can include a column with personal information such as their birthday, their partner's and children's names, and so on. You can also insert notes about their current job, projects and so on.

This list will help you build relationships with a large number of people. They are likely to think of you when they have a need that you could meet. Some of them may also recommend you to others.

While completing this exercise you may realise you no longer remember much about some people whose business cards you have collected. You can overcome this problem in future by writing what you remember about them on the back of the card shortly after meeting them. An even better solution is to enter their contact details and background information into a database. If you have discovered a topic of mutual interest during your conversation, you can send an e-mail to follow up.

How can you help?
People are most likely to hire you if you can solve a problem that is causing them pain. Pain comes in many forms, ranging from toothache to broken-down central heating to lost opportunities if they do not have the right staff. The greater the pain, the greater the urgency and willingness to pay someone to get rid of it. Instead of trying to sell your services all the time, it is better to follow closely what is happening. You can then contact people at just the right time and offer to help.

You may read in the press or on the Web that one of your contacts has been promoted, or that a problem has arisen in their organisation. You can then send them an e-mail or text message, or give them a call. Technology can improve your response time. Search engines such as Google can help you keep track of public announcements. The Alerts function – currently free of charge – allows you to request updates on people and companies, which are sent to you by e-mail. If you re-route them to your mobile phone or BlackBerry, you can react quickly.

Allow a powerful network to form around you
Much has been said on the subject of networking techniques. However, many of us feel uncomfortable about cultivating someone in the hope of getting something from them. This negative feeling is a poor way to start a relationship.

Srikumar Rao teaches a popular course at Columbia, the London Business School and the Haas School of Business at the University of California, Berkeley. He is also a successful author and speaker. Srikumar has a powerful technique for overcoming this problem, which goes as follows:

- Stop trying to cultivate relationships with people you meet, in the hope that they could be helpful to you.

- Next time you meet or hear about someone who is doing something you really admire, stop for a moment. It must be something that moves you. For example, they could be making television documentaries, turning around an ailing business or running a charity that helps violent offenders to lead a normal life. It is highly likely that you and the person you admire have values in common.

- Send them a note or e-mail explaining what moved you and expressing your admiration. Offer to help them in some specific way. Be prepared to go ahead if they accept your offer.

- Your intention is the key. You are not doing this because you want to form a relationship with them. It is because you believe in what they are doing.

- You will be surprised at how often your offer is accepted. Without your even having to try, a powerful network will form around you.

In short, your networking should be aligned with your values. It should also be consistent with your purpose and hence your main archetype.

11

Telling Your Story

We hope you have completed the exercises so far. If so, you will be much clearer about the brand you intend to build. Now you are going to talk to people, what will you say?

Summarise what you do in three seconds
The next person you meet could lead you to a great opportunity. If they ask what you do, you may only have a few seconds to answer. It may be at a social event. Just when you have started talking, you are interrupted by someone who wants you to pass the biscuits. Then the conversation moves on to another topic.

You therefore need a message that is concise and memorable. We call it your *three-second statement.* If you only say you are a headhunter, an accountant or a psychiatrist, the conversation may end there. If you mention *two* activities, at least twice as many people will want to know more. They will pick up on the topic that interests them most.

You can base your three-second statement on your *unique combination*, which we discussed in Chapter 6. If you have already asked the other person a question or two, you can make your statement directly relevant to them. Here are some examples. Each person has chosen two points from his or her unique combination:

- **"I'm a business psychologist with a marketing background."**

  "People often ask what a business psychologist is. The link between psychology and marketing is new to most people. Some of them want to explore it. A lot of people are interested in psychology or marketing – or both."

- **"I'm a banker and a school governor."**

  "Some people are happy talking about banking, particularly if they work in financial services. However, a lot more people have children and talk to me about education. Being a school governor gives me a link with the local community."

- **"I'm the chief executive of a retail business. I'm also on the board of a private equity fund."**

  "Some people want to talk about retail. Everyone has an opinion because we all go shopping. Financial people usually want to talk about private equity."

- **"I'm an account director for an advertising agency. I also do a lot of photography."**

  "Some people want to know which agency I work for. Others ask what kind of photographs I take. The two work well together, because so much advertising is visual. Being a photographer makes me better at advertising, and vice versa."

- **"I'm studying journalism. At the moment I'm getting some work experience."**

  "Many people are interested in journalism. They ask me why I chose it, how I decide what I'm going to write about, and so on."

- **"I'm a headhunter and I write books."**

  "Some people ask 'Can you headhunt me?' or 'What kind of people do you recruit?' They could be interested as a client or as a candidate. Others ask 'What do you write about?' We often get talking about their career."

- **"I'm an accountant.
  I focus on helping small businesses."**

  "Being an accountant isn't unusual, but some people have a tax issue which they ask me about. Many people either know someone who runs their own business or want to start one themselves. Either way, we get talking."

- **"I'm an electrician. I also play the trumpet in a jazz band."**

  "It's an unusual combination for most people, so they tend to remember me. There's a trumpet on my business cards and on the side of my van. My business is called Clarion Electrical."

- **"I'm a dentist. Most of my patients are investment bankers."**

  "Most people like to keep away from dentistry as much as possible, but some are intrigued that I specialise in treating investment bankers. Other medical people are usually happy to talk about dentistry."

Your three-second statement helps to communicate your unique combination and make people remember you. For example, there are plenty of dentists, but we know only one who specialises in investment bankers. That makes her unique and memorable.

EXERCISE G: Your Three-Second Statement

The aim is to catch people's attention and be memorable. Think of two aspects of what you do that could interest other people and are likely to make you unique. Write down one or two sentences, in the style you would use during a casual conversation. Test your three-second statement on friends and family members. Then test it on people you meet for the first time. Make a mental note of what gets their attention and leads to a longer conversation.

Henry's statement was:

"I'm a banker. I do lots of restructuring."

Elisabeth said:

"I'm in sales and marketing. I help companies to grow faster."

Facts tell, stories sell

Most of us find it easier to remember a story than a series of facts. We tell stories about people as a way of illustrating their character or abilities. You can also tell a story about *yourself,* drawing on one of the high points we identified in Chapter 4. It should be a story that illustrates your talents in an authentic way.

Most finance directors in the UK are accountants in dark suits, aged between 30 and 60. Since every business of any size has a finance director, there are thousands of people who fit this description. If you asked them if they were good communicators, practically all of them would say yes. All this makes it difficult for a finance director to stand out from the crowd.

On one occasion John interviewed a finance director whose mother tongue was Cantonese. The candidate mentioned that he had attended an awards ceremony in London where he had interpreted for Jackie Chan, the star of many martial-arts films. This anecdote works very well from a branding point of view. In a sentence or two it tells us that (a) he is bilingual/bicultural, (b) he is probably comfortable in front of a large audience, and (c) he has connections that extend beyond finance. Above all, it makes him *memorable.*

When you pass on anecdotes about yourself, the facts must stand up to scrutiny. Some headhunters have met several people who claim to have launched Haägen-Dazs ice cream. They cannot all be telling the truth. It is more credible to say you were a member of the team that launched it. You can also be specific about your contribution. Given the scale of the project, the most that anyone can say is that they *led* the team. The aim is to encourage powerful word-of-mouth advertising, rather than expose yourself to ridicule. If you are an upwardly mobile executive, it is better to focus on what your *team* achieved, rather than take all the credit yourself.

Although many people enjoy hearing stories, they still want straight answers to their questions. If someone asks "Can you do X?", it is best to say yes or no. You can then support your statement with an example. If you avoid giving straight answers, people may feel that you are hiding something.

It usually helps to mention what you are working on right now, particularly if it is a high-profile project. It shows you are in demand. Beware of appearing *too* busy, however, just in case someone has another project for you.

What to say if you're looking for work

If you have no work right now, it is important to be positive while making it clear that you are looking for a new opportunity. Here are some examples:

- "I finished at XYZ Co. a month ago. I'm now looking for another full-time role in marketing. In the meantime I'm helping a friend to launch a new product."

- "I used to be a financial controller at ABC Hotels. I'm now looking for new opportunities in property and manufacturing."

- "I was IT director of FGH until a couple of months ago. There's a shortage of IT people at the moment, so I've been looking at several opportunities."

It is better not to talk about why you left your old company unless the question comes up. In case it does, it is worth preparing a truthful answer that shows you have moved on with a positive attitude. For example:

- "Last year the overheads doubled just before the revenues halved. Half the staff had to leave, including me, so I'm now looking for another opportunity."

- "After the merger, our whole department relocated to Geneva. I couldn't move my family, so I'm now looking for a similar role in this area."

It is best to keep it brief. The more you talk about the past, the less attractive you will be to new employers, who are interested in what you can do for *them*. However, at some point you may be asked to summarise your career. You must be clear about who you are and what you want to do. For example:

- "I've spent most of my career in property, most recently as a business development director for North America. Now I want to *run* a business."

- "I've managed businesses in several industries and have led change programmes. Now I'm planning to join a management consultancy firm."

It is best to be specific, but not prescriptive, about what you are looking for. The person you are talking to may think of someone you should meet, and tell you right away. Equally, they may bump into someone a few days later and then get back in touch with you.

Respect your heritage and build on it
Personal brands have a lot in common with luxury brands. In both cases customers will pay a premium for top quality, unique features and a distinct brand identity. There

is a magic formula for luxury that can also be applied to personal brands. Successful luxury brands combine two attributes: *heritage* and *contemporary appeal*. As far as heritage is concerned, they tell you about the craftsmen who have been working away for a century or more. They also underline their contemporary appeal by employing talented designers who tap into the latest trends.

HIGH		
H **E** **R** **I** **T** **A** **G** **E**	OLD-FASHIONED	SUCCESSFUL LUXURY BRAND
	IRRELEVANT	TRENDY
LOW		
	LOW	**HIGH**
	CONTEMPORARY APPEAL	

Many unsuccessful luxury brands have one attribute or the other, but not both. Some project their heritage, but the design is not contemporary. Customers dismiss these brands as *old-fashioned.* You might inherit one of their products from your grandparents, but you would not buy any of them. Other unsuccessful brands have well-known designers but discard their heritage. Their products have no consistent theme – they just follow fashion. The quality is not great either. The brand becomes *trendy* and ends up competing with other fashion items. It is unable to command a premium. Brands that have neither heritage nor contemporary appeal are *irrelevant* to consumers of luxury goods.

By combining heritage and contemporary appeal, successful luxury brands become far more successful and profitable than those that are old-fashioned or trendy. The same principle applies to your personal brand. Potential employers and clients are reassured by where you worked and what you did earlier in your career. It is part of your heritage. Throughout your working life, colleagues, headhunters, journalists and others will say "He began his career with ABC company" or "she practised law before starting a chain of restaurants". Even if you are now doing something completely different, your heritage gives people an indication of the quality of your work. It has a big impact on how they perceive you. It affects their willingness to buy from you, work with you or invest in your business.

There are two big mistakes to avoid. The first is to discard your heritage. This gives your clients less re-assurance, making you less valuable to them. It is even worse to *criticise* your old firm, particularly if your contract was terminated and you feel sore about it. Negativity is a big turn-off and is bad for your brand.

The second mistake is to stop improving and updating your brand. After a while you lose contemporary appeal and are regarded as old-fashioned. Saying "When I was at IBM we did it this way" only works for a short time. It is essential to innovate, so that what you are doing *now* is even better than what you did at IBM. The market moves on. You and your brand should do the same.

Archetypes help to ensure that you tell your story in the right way

By now you have probably chosen one or two archetypes that you are going to evoke consistently. It is equally important *not* to evoke other archetypes that could dilute your brand. For example, as a business psychologist, David usually evokes the Magician – he helps people to transform their career. However, he often starts off by evoking the Caregiver, so people feel comfortable and realise they can trust him. If we now refer to some of the other archetypes, we can see how evoking them would be bad for his brand:

- The Explorer: too uncertain. They want solutions, not endless possibilities.
- The Innocent: too ethereal. They want help in dealing with reality.
- The Jester: too flippant. They expect David to take their problem seriously.
- The Lover: inappropriate for a psychologist's relationship with a client!
- The Outlaw: too risky. They do not want a psychologist who breaks the rules.
- The Ruler: too controlling. They want the freedom to find their own way.

Archetypes can help you choose the right metaphor

You can also use *metaphor* – where one thing symbolises another – to tell your story. People often do so unconsciously. However, it can work strongly for or against your brand, so it is worth thinking things through.

One example is military metaphors. They can be useful when you are talking about launching a marketing *campaign* or *capturing* a share of the market. If you were a chief executive talking to shareholders, you might say "We will wipe out the competition" or "Our marketing offensive will capture X per cent of the market". This can work well if everything else you say and do evokes the Hero. However, it can clash badly with other archetypes such as the Caregiver. Now imagine that you are the chief executive of a chain of private clinics and you promise to wipe out the competition! In this case the Heroic vocabulary clashes with the Caregiver archetype. Metaphors only work if the archetype they evoke is consistent with the brand you are building.

The other danger of metaphors is that they can descend into clichés, particularly in written material. This makes you look unimaginative. We know one consultancy firm whose website exhorted readers to "Think outside the box!" Although they wanted to tell people they were creative, the way they did so was unoriginal.

Metaphors work best if used sparingly. When talking to an individual or a small group, you can choose a metaphor that will work with *them.* If you were saving a company from disaster and wished to evoke the Hero, you might tell the staff and shareholders that the company was "fighting for survival". This could inspire them to support you. In a more stable situation you might evoke the Ruler. You could say you were "strengthening the foundations", thereby encouraging people to place their trust in you. If you were evoking the Creator, you could say you were "building a platform for growth". This would help to attract people who wanted to be part of something new and exciting.

EXERCISE H: Metaphors at Work

Think about the main archetype you wish to evoke in your work. Which metaphors would reinforce your brand identity? Which would help you to extend your brand?

Henry decided that artistic metaphors worked best for him. This is what he says about the process:

"I work towards a consensus by asking people to imagine a picture of the way they want their organisation to be. Then I ask them which elements are missing from the picture. Just like any artist, I am in charge. I control the information I receive and apply it in layers like an oil painting until it starts to feel right. Often the parts come together and I have something I can almost frame. I usually start with an outline of what I want to achieve and that helps me to identify the parts of the picture I need to spend more time on."

The Caregiver and Ruler archetypes come across clearly. Although Henry involves people in his painting, he keeps control of it. Elisabeth loves architecture, so she finds it an easy metaphor to use in her work. In this example she evokes both the Caregiver and the Hero:

"I build relationships the way well-known architects build eye-catching buildings: standing out from the crowd, pushing back the boundaries, taking risks. People remember me because I'm not afraid to

> speak out for what I believe needs to happen. I build some strong foundations with stakeholders before I present radical ideas. I get existing clients to mention me. I structure what I'm going to say, based firmly on the brief, but I remain true to myself and I'm never afraid to disagree."

Words that evoke your archetype

By choosing your words carefully, you can evoke your main archetype and strengthen your brand identity. Here are the 12 archetypes, with words you can use to evoke them.

- **The Caregiver** – Care. Serve. Altruism. Compassion. Generosity. Help others. Protect. Comfort. Nurture. Saint. Parent. Helper. Supporter. Love. Affection. Empathy. Commitment. Friendly. Concern.

- **The Creator** – Create. Innovate. Self-expression. Non-conformist. Vision. Artistic. Imagination. Invent. Inspiration. Daydream. Fantasy. Decoration. Experiment. Unconventional. Beauty. Aesthetic.

- **The Explorer** – Explore. Discover. Seek. Wander. Find out. Adventure. Individual. Pioneer. Freedom. Risk. Fearless. Experience. Curious.

- **The Hero** – Courage. Prove your worth. Challenge. Competition. Strong. Powerful. Determination. Persevere. Prevail. Rescue. Discipline. Character. Turnaround.

- **The Innocent** – Purity. Goodness. Happy. Happiness. Simple. Paradise. Cleanse. Honesty. Hope. Child. Rebirth.

- **The Jester** – Fun. Humour. Games. Play. Laughter. Live for the moment. Spontaneous. Impulsive. Have a great time. Jokes. Joy. Enjoyment. Tricks. Pranks. Clown. Entertainment. Comedy. Fool. Mischievous. Manipulative. Playful. Light-hearted. Break the rules. Party. Ridiculous. Outrageous. Clever.

- **The Lover** – Love. Sensual. Sensory. Pleasure. Intimacy. Beautiful. Handsome. Romance. Relationship. Attractive. Passion. Erotic. Sex. Gratitude. Appreciation. Commitment. Friendship. Relationship. Care. Affection. Seduction. Venus. Heart to heart. Indulge. Kiss. Gorgeous. Bliss. Pampering. Caress. Togetherness.

- **The Magician** –Transform. Change. Spiritual. Fundamental laws of how things work. Magical. Make dreams come true. Find win-win solutions. Realise a vision. The inner determines the outer. As above, so below. Synchronicity. Meaningful coincidences. Charisma. Hunches. The experience of flow. Miracles.

- **The Ordinary Guy/Girl** – Connect. Belong. Fit in. Blend in. Friendship. The boy or girl next door. Good neighbour. Down-to-earth. Humanitarian. Functional. Straightforward. Wholesome. Normal. Team spirit. The underdog. Everyday life. Unpretentious.

- **The Outlaw** – Break the rules. Revenge. Rebellion.
  Disrupt. Destroy. Shock. Outrageous. Radical.
  Counterculture. Unacceptable. The dark side.
  Unconventional. Outsider. Independent thinking.

- **The Ruler** – Rule. Control. Order. Commanding.
  Authority. Power. Substance. Impressive. Leadership.
  Taking charge. Organise. Policies. Procedures. Boss.
  Responsible. Manager. Administrator. Status. Prestige.
  Establishment. Hierarchy. Supervise. Success.
  Importance. Godlike. Stature. Exclusive. Insider.
  Privilege. Royalty. King. Queen. Empire. Emperor.
  Standards. Structure.

- **The Sage** – Understand. Information. Knowledge.
  Wisdom. Truth. Objectivity. Expert. Advisor. Mentor.
  Teacher. Detect. Father. Mother.

Make sure your speech and gestures evoke your archetype

Some common habits of speech clash with the speaker's
archetype and weaken his or her brand. One example
is *up-speak:* the voice rises at the end of each sentence,
making statements sounds like questions. If you are a
senior executive evoking the Ruler, this will detract from
your brand by injecting a note of uncertainty. Likewise,
if you normally evoke the Hero, any uncertainty will
discourage people from following you.

You may have been taught not to move your hands
when you speak. We beg to differ. If you use your hands
to support what you are saying, it gives you more energy
and enthusiasm. Singers do this in recording studios,
even when no one is looking except for the producer. Your
gestures simply need to support your message rather than
distracting people from it.

Does your CV convey your purpose?

If you are following a well-trodden path, your CV may speak for itself. A logical progression from one blue-chip employer to another can tell the story well enough. However, many careers do not follow this pattern. If you have changed role or sector, your CV can start to look messy, particularly if you have done some consultancy work or started your own business. Many employers and recruitment consultants are looking for someone with a standard background to do a standard job – a square peg for a square hole. If you have an unusual combination of skills and experience, you are unlikely to fit. The odds of success are low if you are competing against candidates who *do* have the standard background.

However, if you package your experience correctly, and evoke your archetype, you can make yourself much more attractive to an employer who wants what you have to offer. You can do this by inserting a paragraph in your covering letter – or at the top of your CV – describing your *purpose.* It will help people to understand the central theme of your career. For example, Richard began his career in sales and marketing and then moved into general management. Here is the statement from the top of his CV which expresses his purpose:

"I transform businesses and help them fulfil their potential. I have done so as a long-term employee and on short-term contracts. I have worked in luxury goods, fast-moving consumer goods, property and services."

This statement ties his experience together and makes it easy to understand. We do not recommend you talk about Jungian archetypes – you may attract unwelcome attention from psychiatrists. All you need to do is *evoke* your main archetype through your vocabulary and behaviour. In the example above, the key word is *transform.* It evokes the Magician, which is Richard's main archetype. When he joins a business as managing director, it is usually in reasonable shape. However, it could be doing a lot better. He transforms it and helps it to fulfil its potential. Richard does not naturally evoke the Hero, since the businesses he runs do not need rescuing. Equally, he does not evoke the Ruler. They are usually subsidiaries of larger companies and have adequate controls in place.

When Richard describes the companies he has transformed, he becomes animated and enthusiastic. This is usually a sign that someone is describing their purpose. By expressing his purpose at the top of his CV, he will find it easier to attract people who want their company transforming. Employers who want an Heroic turnaround are unlikely to invite him for interview. The same goes for people who want to Rule their empire without major changes. This will save him time. He can focus on the opportunities he finds genuinely exciting.

Now we have discussed how you tell your story, it is time to talk about your appearance.

12

Your Appearance

The famous people we mentioned in Chapter 8 communicated their purpose and their archetype through their appearance. You can do the same.

Pierre the business development director is a good example. He grew up on both sides of the Atlantic and speaks several languages. He is now based in London, where he works for a company that evokes the Ruler. His favourite archetype is the Explorer. It happens to fit his job, which is to explore European markets for opportunities to expand the business.

Most of his colleagues have dark leather briefcases that are consistent with the Ruler. Pierre, however, carries a brown leather shoulder bag with a large flap and a buckle. He also has a small suitcase with wheels, which is handy when he travels by train or by plane. Both are consistent with the Explorer. Pierre chose his luggage before he learned about archetypes. However, he recalls that his new boss commented favourably on his shoulder bag at the interview.

His office is neutral, except for a map of the countries he is currently exploring. At home he has lots of books about Africa and other faraway places. If Pierre keeps some of them in his office it will help him to evoke the Explorer. So could souvenirs from distant continents or a model of the space shuttle. Photos of hot air balloons gliding over dramatic landscapes would have a similar effect.

Since Pierre's role has been created recently, colleagues sometimes ask what he is *for*. His accessories and surroundings help to answer that question. They support his efforts to expand the business into new markets.

Your clothing can evoke your archetype
In choosing your clothes, it is worth thinking about the archetype you are going to evoke, both within your organisation and externally. Maybe you are the founder of a technology company and have brilliant ideas which others help to implement. If so, you may wish to evoke the Creator, using highly original clothing. You might also choose an unusual hairstyle, as Albert Einstein did. If you are breaking the rules within your industry, you may wish to evoke the Outlaw, deliberately failing to conform to the accepted dress code in your sector.

Although ties are becoming scarcer, they tend to reappear when people are raising money or looking for a job. There are good reasons for this. If you are raising money, formal attire helps to evoke the Ruler. Investors and/or lenders will be more confident that you will keep the business firmly under control and protect their interests. There is also a cyclical aspect to men's clothing. According to Alan Flusser, the American designer and author, men have historically opted for ties during periods of economic uncertainty. Sales of ties usually go up during financial downturns. If you want to keep your job, it is a good time to evoke the Ruler more than you might do otherwise.

In the 1950s many office workers wore a suit and tie to work every day. This evoked the Ruler, which was appropriate for members of a hierarchy. However, it is now common for staff to wear smart-casual (or not-so-smart casual) clothes. In some companies the rulers wear open-necked shirts and chinos. Their underlings wear suits and ties and may be regarded as old-fashioned, perhaps even evoking the Jester.

Whatever the dress code in your organisation, you can choose to wear clothes that also evoke your archetype. For example, if everyone in your office wears smart casual, you can evoke the Outlaw by including something outrageous in your wardrobe. You can evoke the Ruler by wearing an expensive accessory that is in short supply. Hence investment bankers and hedge-fund managers in casual clothes often wear expensive mechanical watches, despite being surrounded by electronic gadgetry. A Creator in a smart-casual environment could wear something at the forefront of fashion, thus remaining innovative in a conformist environment. It is good to dress stylishly, whether the style is conservative, casual or flamboyant.

Henry's clothing reflects the long period he has spent in banking. He tends to wear a dark grey or blue suit, with a pin-striped shirt and a silk tie. These days he usually does not wear a tie in the office, although he always has one ready for an unexpected meeting with a client. He tends not to stand out from his colleagues, preferring to merge into the background by wearing the banking uniform.

Elisabeth's approach is different. Since she is in sales and marketing, it helps to stand out and be memorable. She wears a high-quality scarf and shoes that make her stand out from the crowd. However, she has recently toned down her colours. She now wears a tailored business suit, reflecting her intention to move into senior management.

EXERCISE I: Appearances

Next time you are waiting in a reception area, observe people's appearance as they enter and leave. Which archetypes do they evoke? Look and listen for clues as to why they are there. How well does their archetype evoke their purpose?

Now we have discussed your appearance, it is time to talk about your behaviour.

13

Your Behaviour

Our behaviour is shaped by the way we see the universe and our place within it. In this chapter we will describe an approach that is thousands of years old but is new to most people.

Many of us live our lives on the basis of an unspoken assumption: that we are separate from everyone and everything around us. This is known as *duality* – a split into two. *Dualistic* thinking pervades our lives. We divide the universe into pairs of opposites: them and us, black and white, good and evil, and so on. This habit is so ingrained that we may never think about it. However, *all* conflict is based on duality. It happens at work, in our social lives and in the strife between religious and ethnic groups. Duality leads people to see themselves as separate from each other and from the rest of the universe. It is sometimes described as the *illusion of separation.* As Albert Einstein put it, "a human being is part of the whole, called by us 'universe', a part limited in time and space. He experiences himself, his thoughts and feelings as something separated from the rest – a kind of optical delusion of his consciousness."

Many people's attempts at marketing themselves are based on dualistic thinking. They try very hard to *get* something – and it shows. It often makes their efforts counterproductive. For example, they pester their contacts in the hope of being rewarded with a job or an assignment. They send the same CV several times to any headhunter or employer they know. Unfortunately this makes them look needy, which is bad news when building any kind of relationship. The underlying message is: "Please give me a job or project to work on. Otherwise I'll starve." If you ask them if they feel comfortable doing all of this, most will say no. Fortunately there is a better way.

Everyone and everything is connected
This view goes back thousands of years and is known as *unity*. It was expressed in the *Upanishads,* usually translated as 'at the feet of some master'. They were passed on by word of mouth over many generations and were written down from around 600 BC onwards. One of the most famous verses is this: "In the beginning, there was mere being, one without a second" *(Chhandôgya-Upanishad).* In other words, everything is part of the whole. The practice of yoga, translated as *union,* belongs to this tradition. As the Brazilian author Paulo Coelho puts it, *all things are one.*

In many ways this is a convincing description of reality. In physical terms, every cell in our body is replaced within seven years. Ninety-eight per cent of the atoms in our body were not there a year ago. We are not physically the same person at all. Even in the very short term, during a face-to-face conversation, we will exchange molecules with the other person, and with our surroundings, as each of us breathes in and out.

Intellectually, we are more closely linked than we sometimes imagine, since there is clearly a degree of shared consciousness among human beings. One example is when scientists working independently in different parts of the world discover something simultaneously. Rupert Sheldrake, the biologist, goes a step further. He argues that all natural systems, from crystals to human society, inherit a collective memory that influences their form and behaviour.

In *emotional* and *spiritual* terms, we interact with everyone around us. We readily talk about the *atmosphere* in a room full of people, or the *feeling* we had about what was going on during a meeting. The social links are obvious. Most of what we do requires the close involvement of other people. For example, it would be virtually impossible to do our jobs, raise children or perform most pieces of music without other people's cooperation. We rely on our environment for many things, from clean air to healthy food, to living without fear of some natural disaster destroying our homes. All human activity has an impact on our environment. It is only a matter of time before we feel the effect of our actions.

In the second half of the twentieth century, physicists began pursuing the idea that everyone and everything is connected. In 1964 Bell's Theorem stated that "all objects and events in the cosmos are inter-connected with one another and respond to one another's change of state". David Bohm, one of Albert Einstein's colleagues, took it a step further, describing an "invisible field that holds all of reality together, a field that possesses the property of knowing what is happening everywhere at once".

There is scientific evidence to support this view. An experiment led by Alain Aspect in 1982 demonstrated a connection between subatomic particles that were far apart. They appeared to communicate faster than the speed of light, which – according to Einstein – is the maximum speed at which a physical signal can travel. Given the demands of scientific proof, it could be a long time before the connectedness of the universe is fully demonstrated under laboratory conditions. However, this and other experiments are consistent with the principle of unity.

Karma

Unity has major implications for the way you build your brand. Since you are connected with everyone and everything, whatever you think, say or do will affect everyone, including you. When you serve one person, you are serving everyone, including yourself. This brings us to the *Law of Karma.*

Whatever you do comes back to you in some form.

In other words, *what goes around comes around.* The Law of Karma is also known as the *law of cause and effect.* (Contrary to popular belief, karma has nothing to do with being calm. It just sounds similar in English.)

If you focus on *serving* people, rather than trying to get something from them, good things will come back to you sooner or later. This idea is common to many religions and philosophies. In the New Testament, St Paul wrote that "A man reaps what he sows." The Dhammapada, in the Buddhist tradition, says that "If a man speaks or acts with an impure mind, suffering follows him as the wheel of the cart follows the beast that draws the cart... If a man speaks or acts with a pure mind, joy follows him as his own shadow." According to the Koran, "If any does good, the reward to him is better than his deed."

Since there is no way of knowing *when* or *how* the effect of your actions will come back to you, you do not need anything from the person you are serving right now. Good things are just as likely to come back to you via someone else. For example, this can happen when your reputation for serving people attracts new customers. A saleswoman might give helpful advice to Mr A, telling him *not* to buy her product because it will not meet his needs. Then A recommends her to Mr B, who becomes a customer. Equally, if the saleswoman were to mislead Mr A, Mr B would soon find out. She would lose potential customers, starting with B.

Sometimes the delay between giving and receiving is unexpectedly short. During an economic downturn a few years ago, John was invited to give a talk to a large group of business school graduates. The theme was how to get a job via headhunters. Most people in the audience were either unemployed or feared they would be soon. He explained as clearly as he could how they should approach executive search firms. The next speaker – from a large, blue-chip company – explained how he and his colleagues went about hiring people. He also mentioned that he was having trouble filling a senior position. Within a short while he had hired John and his team to solve the problem.

Karma is not only a question of what you *do*. What you *think* and *say* is also important. Your *intention* towards other people must be positive. Your thoughts, speech and actions will then be aligned. You will also feel good, which will make you more attractive to others, including customers, clients and colleagues. Everyone will benefit, including you.

People sometimes object that the motivation is selfish, since you expect to benefit at some point. However, this objection is itself dualistic – based on the illusion that each of us is separate. Once you see yourself as part of the whole, both giving and receiving become natural and enjoyable. They are effectively the same thing: the universe is giving to and receiving from itself.

EXERCISE J: Unity

As you walk down the street or travel on public transport, see yourself in other people. What are they thinking about? How do they feel?

Put yourself in the shoes of people you meet or speak to on the phone, or who contact you by e-mail. How do they feel? What do they need? How can you help?

EXERCISE K: Your Behaviour

Here is a list of questions about how you behave towards other people. It is not a scorecard. Even if it were, no one would score a hundred per cent. You may already be excellent in some respects. There may also be areas where you could strengthen your brand quickly by making some improvements.

- How quickly and thoroughly do I return phone calls and reply to e-mails?

- Am I approachable, or do people have to judge my mood before they talk to me?

- Do I do what I have promised? (If not, it may be better to make fewer promises, giving you time to fulfil those you do make.)

- Do I help people spontaneously? (For example, you might spot a potential opportunity for them in a newspaper and tell them about it.)

- Does my behaviour fit my archetype? (If you evoke the Caregiver, are you caring at all times, or could people conclude that you don't care? If the Ruler is your archetype, do you evoke it consistently, giving people reassurance?)

Henry and Elisabeth gave this short questionnaire to people who knew them well. Henry discovered that people found him lax in returning phone calls. Some said he had been quite brusque the first time they had met him. However, once they had got to know him he had become much warmer. He praised people spontaneously and did his best to help them. They identified the Caregiver as his main archetype, followed by the Ruler. They included the Ruler because of the unapproachable, even arrogant, stance he sometimes adopted.

Henry realised he felt uneasy when he met people for the first time. Some of them interpreted this as arrogance. He worked with a coach who made a video of him in action with his team and then helped him to become more open with people, establishing eye contact in a friendly manner. He also developed his listening skills, so he could build a stronger rapport more quickly.

Elisabeth's contacts tended to identify her as the Creator rather than the Hero. They noted her determination to be herself and get her own way, convincing those around her that she was right. She recognised that this perception could hinder her progress in a large organisation. People could see her as more detached than she wished to be. She realised that she needed to listen more and involve others. This would help her to take on more responsibility.

Once you begin to understand how other people perceive you, it becomes much easier to adapt your behaviour, so you can fulfil your potential. However, there is another dimension that is at least as important. *Presence* is the subject of our next chapter.

14

Presence

Some people have a strong presence. You can feel it when you are with them. They establish a rapport with you. They attract people they respect as colleagues.

What is presence? One aspect is giving you their complete attention – literally being present. They are with you in the *here and now* – not in the past or the future, or in some other place. Many successful business people, entertainers and politicians are good at remaining in the present. Here is one newspaper's description of a well-known entrepreneur: "It is as if you are standing outside a building with one small window. He opens it and looks out, just to talk to you." If someone is present *with you*, they give their full attention to what you are saying and doing, and what you may be thinking and feeling. Their presence enables them to connect with everyone they meet.

We can also understand presence when we experience a lack of it. Some people are *not* present when they communicate. The words come out of their mouths, but they are somewhere else. If you watch people during a meeting, you can see that some are not present at all.

We all have distracting thoughts. A person of average intelligence absorbs spoken information six times faster than they speak. If you are highly intelligent, you will have even more time to be distracted. You may find yourself thinking about how you are going to respond. All this gets in the way of communication. It is not enough for you to listen. The other person wants to *feel* listened to. They can tell if you are listening to them openly. If you do so, you can build a strong rapport with them.

One of the best techniques for remaining in the present was developed in Asia thousands of years ago. It is sometimes called *reconnecting with the senses.* Using one or more of your senses, you place your attention on something in the present. This keeps you in the here and now. The continuous stream of thoughts begins to die down, and your mind becomes clearer. Once you have practised this exercise a few times, you will be able to remain present every time you communicate with someone. It will make you much more effective.

EXERCISE L: Being Present

This exercise takes five to ten minutes. It is best if someone reads it out while you close your eyes and listen. Alternatively, you can record it and play it back. Whoever reads it out should leave big pauses between each paragraph.

"Sit upright on your chair, remaining completely relaxed. Keep your feet flat on the floor and as far apart as your hips. Keep your hands open in front of you and rest them on your thighs. Close your eyes. Allow your body to relax, letting go of any tension.

Feel where you are now: the clothes touching your skin, the weight of your body on the chair, the air on your face and hands.

Become aware of taste and smell. Listen as far as possible into the distance, beyond the sounds nearby. Listen carefully for a while.

Let go of any mental comments or judgements about the sounds. Rest your attention on the breath as it flows in and out of your body. Do not try to change any of this. Simply allow your attention to rest upon your breath.

Every now and then a thought will arise. If you resist it, it will persist. Just notice it and let it go.

Sense the infinite space stretching in front of you, behind you, above you, below you and on both sides. Remain aware of this for a while.

Open your eyes. Notice the colour and form of the objects around you. Feel the weight of your body on the chair, the air on your face and hands. Remain aware of this for a while ...

As your mind quietens down, you will continue to notice thoughts as they arise. If you rest your attention on the breath, they will leave of their own accord."

It is important to sit upright during this exercise. If you lie down, you may fall asleep, as Henry did the first time he tried it.

This exercise is sometimes called *mindfulness meditation.* You are mindful of the breath, the air on your face and hands, and so on. Most people have to do it several times before it has a major effect. It helps you develop a *quiet mind.* As it says in the *Tao Te Ching,* "Empty yourself of everything. Let the mind become still."

Although it takes effort, it brings many benefits. One of them is a stronger rapport with everyone. They want to feel that you are listening to them. The more carefully you listen, the more you will absorb and the better they will feel about you.

Technology can disrupt your rapport with other people, if you allow it. If you leave your mobile phone or BlackBerry switched on, or keep looking at a computer screen, you cannot give them your full attention. One solution is to take out your mobile and say "I'm going to switch this off now". You then do so and leave it on the table. Many people will follow your example.

Acceptance

Another aspect of presence is *acceptance*. This includes accepting yourself as you are and the situation as it is. You can feel when someone accepts themselves. They are at peace and do not pretend to be anything. They do not judge themselves or other people. They also accept you exactly as you are.

Acceptance is a form of love – it draws people to you. If you accept things as they are, rather than as you think they should be, then you can make appropriate plans and take action. As Deepak Chopra says, "Accept the present, intend the future". Here is an exercise to help you accept.

EXERCISE M: Acceptance

Today I shall accept everything that occurs.

As you go about your daily activities, observe what goes on around you. Notice the way people speak and behave, the weather, the pace at which things happen or don't happen, the thoughts that appear in your mind, and so on.

If you remain in the present you can also observe any judgements as they appear: "she shouldn't have said that", "people shouldn't do that", "what a stupid situation" and so on. However, instead of clinging to them, you can let them go. Don't try to resist them. These judgements are not yours in the first place. You can just let them go.

Imagine you are standing on a bridge, looking down into a river as it rushes past. *If you can observe it, it's not you.* Fairly soon the judgements will vanish. New thoughts may appear. You can let go of them too.

You still *care* about what goes on around you. If you remain in the present you can take the right action at the right time. If a child or a dog runs out into the road, you can intervene immediately. However, whether observing or taking action, you avoid judging. It frees you from negative emotions that sap your energy. It helps you do what needs to be done, at just the right time.

Today I shall accept everything that occurs.

Visualisation

Your presence is also affected by how you feel about yourself, which is largely determined by how you see yourself. As it says in the *Vedas,* written thousands of years ago, *what you see you become.*

The aim of this book is to help you fulfil your potential. It will happen a lot faster if you imagine it vividly *now.* Athletes have been using this technique for decades. It is sometimes referred to as *mental rehearsal.* They lie still on a sofa and visualise themselves winning. They also imagine the sounds, the smells and the physical sensations. The more senses are involved, the more the mind accepts the situation as real. Having repeated this exercise many times, when they compete they automatically do the right thing at the right time. They do not need to recall the visualisation, since it is already stored in their subconscious. While they are competing, it is best if they remain in the present, as we described earlier. Timothy Gallwey put it like this in *The Inner Game of Tennis:* "During such experiences, the mind does not act like a separate entity telling you what you should do or criticizing how you do it. It is quiet; you are 'together', and the action flows as free as a river." This is sometimes described as being *in the zone.*

Mental rehearsal only works if you are rehearsing something that fits your talents and your values. If you are not an Olympic athlete, or physically capable of becoming one, there is no point in mentally rehearsing your gold medal victory. Likewise, we do not recommend that you vividly imagine something that clashes with your values. Whatever you rehearse in your mind should be a natural – if ambitious – extension of who you are.

For example, if you have a talent for starting new businesses, and you believe strongly in alternative energy, then launching a business in that sector could be a natural thing for you to do. It fits both your talents and your values. This will help you to enjoy it and overcome any obstacles. When you mentally rehearse a successful outcome, it will feel real because it fits you.

Mental rehearsal works best if you use all your senses. If you are a budding Olympic athlete, you can see yourself crossing the finishing line, with only press photographers in front of you. You can hear the crowd cheering in the background and your name being announced over the loudspeaker. You can feel the tape on the finishing line breaking across your chest, your feet on the steps of the rostrum and the gold medal being placed over your head. You can even imagine the smell of the sweating bodies around you. Your mind accepts that your intention has already been realised. It is like watching a film that absorbs you completely. Even if the story is fictional, you have strong feelings and beliefs about what you see and hear.

Once your mind has experienced success, the actions come naturally. When you meet people or talk to them on the phone, you will look and sound like the person you intend to be. This can have dramatic results.

Here is an exercise to help you put this into practice. Ideally you should ask someone to read it out to you. Alternatively, you can read it straight through and complete it one step at a time.

EXERCISE N: Mental Rehearsal

Sit quietly with your eyes closed. Rest your attention on the breath flowing slowly in and out of your body. When the random thoughts have died down and you are in the present, keep your eyes gently closed. Picture the scene when what you intend to happen has already happened. Now add one sense at a time:

- Imagine the sound of people's voices. What are they saying to you and what are you saying to them?
- What can you smell?
- How warm is it? How humid?
- Can you feel the wind or the sun against your skin?
- Is anyone touching you?
- Are you touching anyone or anything?
- How do you *feel* about all this?

The more real the image of what you want to happen, and the more positive you feel about it, the better. At the same time, it is essential to be open-minded about *how* it will happen – when, where or with whom. In terms of career goals, your dream may be realised where you are now, in another organisation or even in another country.

Once you have done this exercise a couple of times, it is worth writing down a detailed description of what you intend to happen. This will make the experience even more real. Here is an example, written by an executive in the media sector. He has worked his way up from a sales job to the role of a highly-paid managing director:

Steve's Place – What it Looks, Smells and Feels like

"I take the early train as usual. The journey lets me catch up on my reading, prepare myself and get on top of the all-important detail. I like to have the answers for my boss and all the knowledge to hand. Knowing what's going on and why things are happening is important. After buying a coffee at the local Starbucks, I arrive at the office and the receptionist is as pleasant as ever. What's nice is that even the security staff are pleasant and always have a quick chat about something. It feels warm when I enter the building and everyone is friendly and treated like equals. People chat openly to me about their night out or what they're up to, even though I'm in a relatively senior position. I arrive at my desk and log on. The office is pretty empty as I like to get in and sorted out before people arrive. It feels like arriving home. You want to get through the door, and quickly.

My PA arrives and we have a quick chat about the football from the night before. She is a big Manchester United fan and we regularly text each other the scores. Once logged on she briefs me on everything I need for the day, along with a few hints about anything I've overlooked on the personal side. She gently reminds me that I should be on time this evening as Julie has a committee meeting.

As people arrive and the place fills up, I look around at a very open office. It's tidy and clean. People chat openly to each other. There is a sense of honesty about the place and what's unusual is that everyone is helping each other. My boss comes over for a chat. He is interested in Julie and the family. We have a huge presentation today, but he's taking an interest in me and what's important to me. We eventually get on to talk about the presentation. He asks if it's all fine. I've been working on it for over a week, but I just say I'm confident. He completely trusts me and tells me how good I am and that it couldn't be in better hands. He then goes on to have a chat with my team and everyone else. The place feels lively. It's open and honest and people genuinely want to do their best for me and the organisation as a whole.

It feels like we're building something really special at this company. There is no politics and cliques are out of place. The office is in the centre of town, which is great. There is a fantastic view over the river and Julie and the kids love coming to see me for lunch now and then. Everyone loves seeing them when they come in – even the boss. The culture is really open and one of daily improvement. However, lots of intelligent people work here and mutual respect is well earned. There are daily challenges but people are prepared to help and support each other, mostly working through teams.

When things go wrong there's no blame. Risk is managed well, but the culture is one of non-blame. We all get the best out of each other through a shared responsibility. That's what I like about the boss. He encourages you to do more and take the occasional risk, but equally he'll support you if things don't go as planned. He's really respected and we make a great team. It's a very professional relationship and we're very clear, direct and open with each other. We just know when things are going well or badly.

This is a company that is going places. Growth is the story and we're prepared to take whatever decisions we need to. The structure of the company is very clear and people's responsibilities are even clearer. When there's disagreement or ambiguity, we find the middle ground quickly and professionally. The package is great and the holidays are even better. The real excitement about working here is that it feels like an extension of my life. My wife likes the company. I'm really happy when I go home and am excited about getting in the next morning. There's tons to do – in fact too much – but I just love doing it. Exploring new markets, sourcing new deals and making things happen that contribute enormously to the company's growth.

Every time the company presents our results to our investors, it's really exciting. The sense of anticipation, at every level, is enormous. However, the thing that everyone talks about is how the CEO goes around to say hello and thanks to everyone. It's incredible that he remembers all the names and what people have done."

This visualisation contains lots of detail and expresses how Steve *feels* about the situation, which has helped to make it real for him. After writing it he worked on a number of consultancy assignments before taking a job that closely resembles the one he visualised.

It is also very helpful to collect images of what you really want to happen. You can do this in the form of a folder, a scrapbook or pictures on the wall. The more often you look at them – and the stronger the feelings you have about them – the faster you will attract what you want into your life.

While we were writing this book we ran some workshops to test the material on live audiences. At one of them a New Zealander described how, some years before he met his wife, she had decided that she wanted to get an MBA (Master of Business Administration) from a particular business school. Since she was already in the habit of visualising what she wanted, she ordered a brochure from the school. She then cut out some photos that appealed to her and stuck them on the door of her refrigerator. They showed happy students on the MBA programme a year or two earlier. This lady got her MBA and later met and married our friend the New Zealander. As it turns out, he had been in several of the photographs on the refrigerator!

Visualisation can be unexpectedly powerful. It is important to think big and allow yourself to dream. The tools we have discussed in this chapter will help you do so. As Johann Wolfgang von Goethe famously put it, "Whatever you can do, or dream you can, begin it. Boldness has genius, power and magic in it."

Presence is not easy to pin down. However, we know it when we see it or feel it in someone else. If you remain in the present, accept yourself and others, and have a clear vision, you will develop a stronger presence of your own.

15

Getting Paid

Once someone decides to hire you, the question of money will come up. Some people are squeamish about this. Either they accept whatever they are offered or they ask for very little, for fear of being too expensive. Others are completely unrealistic and ask for more than the job is worth. Pricing is important. It affects your material well-being in the short term and the strength of your brand for years to come. If you are building a top-quality brand, you should probably charge a premium price – more than the average supplier of your type of service.

Maybe you have always had a job and accepted the salary you were offered. This can work well in the early stages of your career. If you are a trainee in a well-regarded company, there may be little sense in trying to negotiate your salary. If you build a reputation for excellent work, your market value will increase and they will pay more just to keep you. You can still check how much you are worth by talking to recruitment consultants or other people in your industry.

Once you reach board level, the ability to transfer from one sector to another tends to increase, so you are likely to be paid the market rate. This is particularly true of chief executives, finance directors, chairmen and non-executive directors. In some countries, if a company is quoted on a stock exchange, a remuneration committee decides how much directors are paid and the details are published in the annual report.

Salaries tend to be most out of line with the market somewhere in the middle of large organisations. If you have been with your employer for years, your remuneration may lag behind what people with similar skills are earning elsewhere. The internal pay scale may also hold you back, even if it bears no relation to the market. Some pay scales have no economic rationale. We know a bank where everyone's salary is partly determined by how many people they manage. This means that senior executives in specialist roles cannot earn what they are worth. Some employers subscribe to salary surveys produced by consultancies, which tell them how much they should pay someone for a particular job. However, even surveys cannot provide a definitive answer, since the sector and location have a big influence. The market rate for the job you do will be affected by many factors not captured in these surveys

If you are self-employed, it is even more important to check market rates, so you know roughly what you could be charging. Whether you receive that amount depends partly on the value clients place on your services. If they believe you add a lot of value, they will pay your fees and recommend you to others.

Whether you are employed or self-employed, you will need to negotiate your remuneration at some point. One of the key concepts is the *Best Alternative to A Negotiated Agreement,* otherwise known as the *BATNA.*

It is discussed at length in *Getting To Yes,* which is listed under Recommended Reading. Both you and the person who wants to hire you have a BATNA. *Their* BATNA is what they would have to pay someone else to do the same work to the same standard. *Your* BATNA is the amount you could earn with another employer or client. The Zone of Possible Agreement – or *ZOPA* – is the gap between the two, as shown in the diagram below.

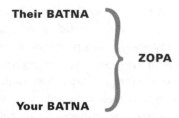

Their BATNA

ZOPA

Your BATNA

Assuming both of you are economically rational, any agreement you reach will be in the ZOPA. If you ask for more than their BATNA, they will be better off hiring someone else. If they offer you less than your BATNA, you will be better off working for someone else.

How do you find out their BATNA? One way is to ask them what their alternatives are and make an estimate of what that will cost them. Maybe they *could* get someone else to do the work. If there are plenty of other people who could do it, you can find out the going rate. If there are only one or two others, you may be able to find out who they are and what they charge. If there is a headhunter involved, you can ask him or her how much such people are likely to be paid. As you build your brand, more people will bid for your services. Your BATNA will rise, narrowing the ZOPA in any negotiations. Your earnings are likely to rise, too. (We hope you will agree that this book has been an excellent investment.)

Not only does the strength of your brand affect the price you can charge, it also works the other way round. The price you charge affects your brand. You could set your price low, in the hope of attracting employers or clients. Ironically, this may put them off. If your price is low, it suggests your BATNA is also low. In other words, no one else is prepared to pay much for your services. Potential customers may infer that you are not very good at what you do.

Since a low asking price can damage your brand, it is much better to work out how much value you can add, and then charge a price that captures some of that value. Above all, you should avoid adding a bit to your costs in order to arrive at your selling price. The management guru Peter Drucker described cost-led pricing as one of the 'five deadly business sins'.

If you are being interviewed by a headhunter, a high salary and bonus can actually work in your favour. Many candidates assume that, if they are highly paid, they are less likely to be interviewed. In fact, the opposite may be true. As with luxury goods, many headhunters find highly priced candidates *reassuringly expensive.* If someone is prepared to pay you that much, you must be good! If you are far cheaper than they would expect, they may start to wonder if there is something wrong with you.

We are not suggesting you *lie* about your remuneration. However, it is good to demonstrate that you know your value in the market. Here are some examples from the distant country of Batnastan, whose currency is the Bat (B):

- "My current base salary is B100. It's low because I'm working for a start-up. The founders have also given me 5% of the shares. I've recently been considering opportunities with a base salary of around B200, and a bonus of 30% to 50%."

- "I've just come back from an overseas posting where my base salary was B400. However, some of that was danger money – most people don't want to live and work there. The packages I've been considering in Batnastan are in the range of B200 to B300."

- "My current base salary is B100. However, I'm flexible about the salary in my next job, provided I do well on my shares if the business succeeds.

If you have done your homework, you will know your BATNA and have some idea of your employer's or client's BATNA. You can now reach an agreement somewhere in the ZOPA.

Where you end up is largely a question of tactics. Imagine you are negotiating your salary with a new employer. You have been interviewed by several other companies and know that you could earn B200 with one of them. You have also done your homework and believe that this particular employer would pay up to B300 for your combination of skills and experience. You believe that, if you asked them for more than B300, they would be better off transferring someone from another country to do your job. Alternatively, they could divide your role in two and pay two people B150 each. To sum up, your BATNA is B200 and theirs is B300, as shown in the diagram below.

In theory you could end up anywhere in the ZOPA between B200 and B300. If you ask for B300 and they offer

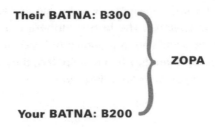

Their BATNA: B300

ZOPA

Your BATNA: B200

B200, you will probably end up somewhere in the middle. Splitting the difference at B250 could satisfy both parties. However, if you move quickly and ask for B300 *in writing*, this can exert a powerful influence on the final outcome. Studies show that agreement is usually reached close to the first price which is mentioned and written down. One possible reason is that the person who makes the first move has done his or her homework more thoroughly than the other party. If you know exactly what your potential employer wants you to do, and how else they could get it done, you will know their BATNA. Most employers would find it more difficult to work out *your* BATNA. They could ask you your current salary, but you might be underpaid. In that case your BATNA is the highest salary you could earn elsewhere. However, they may not have the time or inclination to find all this out. If asked, you can tell your prospective employer what other companies are likely to offer you.

During salary negotiations with a new company, their pay structure may work in your favour. If they have a standard rate for someone in your role, they may offer it to you without any negotiation. If it is significantly higher than your current salary, you may just accept it.

While these discussions are going on, it helps to keep things in perspective. The best remuneration package is one that works for you *and* your employer. If you do an even better job than they had anticipated, they will tend to increase your pay in order to keep you.

16

Becoming More Visible

Once you know who you are and where you are going, it is time to become more visible. There are simple things you can do right away. Later on we will talk about more ambitious ways of putting yourself on the map.

Business cards
Both authors of this book have attended conferences – even networking events – where people have turned up with no business card. Some of them say "give me your card and I'll e-mail you my contact details". Very few do so. It is easy to stand out in this environment. All you need is a clear business card which gives your full contact details, including your phone numbers and your e-mail address. It should also remind people of who you are and what you do.

Most business cards are impersonal, with just a name, a title and a company. If you have any say in the design, it is worth leaving a space on the front so you can write on them when you give them to people. For example, you can write 'PTO' on the front and then write a message on the back to remind them of what you do or the topic you discussed. You can also write the address of your personal website or your page on a social networking site.

Your e-mail address

It is best if your e-mail address begins with your first name. That way, if people have not contacted you for a while, they may find your e-mail address right away when they type your first name into a blank e-mail. Only use a nickname in your e-mail address if you also use it in business.

Some people's e-mail addresses begin with their spouse's name, the name of their cottage in the countryside or some unfathomable combination of numbers and letters. Any of these could lose you a potential client or employer. They may spend time trawling through their 'deleted' folder, searching for an old message from you. More likely, they will give up looking.

If you have a common surname, you can use your e-mail address to remind people of who you are and what you do. Jean Smith is a copy writer who left a large advertising agency to go freelance. She now writes material for brochures and websites. Her e-mail address is *jeansmithwriter@yahoo.co.uk*.

Sending e-mails

E-mail is a good way to stay in touch and is less intrusive than phone calls. If your message has avoided the spam folder and is sitting in someone's in-box, they can read it whenever they want. However, many of us receive e-mails that we delete unread. People are more likely to read yours if you personalise them. It helps if your e-mail address contains your full name. Otherwise you can include it in the subject box. For example: *Update from Sally Jones.*

There are some useful online services for managing your e-mail lists. These include *Your Mailing List Provider,* at *ymlp.com*, and *coollist.com*. There is also *topica.com,* which is intended for small businesses. Sites such as these enable you to mail-merge e-mails to your contacts. You can then send Fred an e-mail which begins 'Dear Fred' rather than 'Dear All' or 'Hi'. Fred is much more likely to pay attention.

Your Web presence
Everyone has a Web strategy for their brand. Usually it is a passive one – do nothing. However, the information may be out of date or inaccurate. It is time to check your presence on the Web.

EXERCISE O: Who are you on the Web?

Type your full name, in inverted commas (" "), into a search engine such as Google. If the first page of results leads to a website with your e-mail address or phone number, that is an excellent start.

Now look at what has been written about you, and the context. Is this the brand image you wish to project? Will employers and clients be attracted by what they read?

It is hard to be visible if your name is a common one such as Janet Jones or Raj Patel. One solution is to make sure you are mentioned in the context of what you do. If your name is John Smith and you are an architect, will people find you if they type "John Smith" and "architect" into Google?

There may be nothing about you, but plenty about a namesake who is a notorious criminal. If you put correct information about yourself on the Web, it will start to crowd out the rest.

Some people are only visible while they remain with their employer. Then they vanish. Even chief executives can disappear once they leave their job. Some recruiters will make an effort to track you down. Others will give up within minutes. Make sure you are easy to find!

Social networking sites

If you want to establish a basic presence on the Web, you can use a social networking site such as Facebook. Anyone who enrols can find you by typing your name into the search function. LinkedIn (*linkedin.com*) and Plaxo (*plaxo.com*) operate in a similar way and include people from a wide range of occupations. More and more recruitment consultants are using these two sites to track down candidates. Some occupations, such as creatives in the advertising sector, have their own websites. These can make you more visible without telling the world that you are looking for a new job. Recruiters will still find you. It is important to choose carefully, ensuring you appear on sites that reflect your values, interests and career ambitions.

Consider setting up a personal website

If you are self-employed, you probably want people to find and contact you. Potential clients may expect you to have a website and assume you are no good if you do not. If you are a media star, a website will help your fans to follow your progress without getting too close. You can also use it to sell CDs, books or merchandise.

Not everyone wants a website. Some angel investors prefer to keep a low profile. It helps them to avoid being mobbed by entrepreneurs seeking finance. Certain financial advisors do the same – it adds to their mystique. Some salaried employees shudder at the thought of setting up a website. They fear it will smack of self-promotion and send the wrong message to their boss. One solution is to appear on another site for a trade association, an industry body or a charity. If you are a non-executive director, it will give you another opportunity to increase your presence on the Web. Researchers in executive search firms look carefully at board members' profiles. As ever, you will be judged by the company you keep.

You can use your website to communicate your unique combination of skills and experience through the text and the illustrations. Your brand identity is more subtle, but no less important. Imagine you are a medical specialist who cures back injuries. The Magician may be your natural archetype. We are not advocating a photograph of you wearing a pointed hat and waving a wand. However, your website will be more powerful if the vocabulary and content evoke the Magician. You could include a page of tips for people you have cured, to help them stay healthy. This will reinforce the message that you make the problem disappear and never return. If you use Magical words such as *transform*, it will help to strengthen your brand identity.

If you are a fitness coach or personal trainer, the Hero is an obvious archetype for you to evoke on your website. You could have pictures of muscular men and women straining every sinew in pursuit of glory. However, that may not reflect what you do for your clients. Many people hire a personal trainer to make them stick to an exercise regime, so they lose weight and get fit. In other words, they want the Ruler. You could evoke the Ruler by having pictures of slim, athletic men and women in suits, striding up the steps to the entrance of a large corporation, with an architrave supported by Doric columns. You could include guidelines for healthy eating and exercise planners that people can download as a PDF.

If appropriate, you can mention your existing clients. The stronger their brands, the more yours will benefit. Links to other websites are crucial. They give people a reason to keep visiting your site and use it as a point of reference. When linking your website to others, make sure the connection enhances your brand. The quality of the sites, and the values they express, should be consistent with your own.

The more useful you make your website, the more likely people are to add it to their *favourites* list. You can also set up a site for a particular project. Clifford Thurlow did this when he wrote a book called *Making Short Films*. The website has become popular among media students and would-be filmmakers. See *www.making-short-films.com.* It has also increased the traffic on Clifford's own site.

Unless you are an accomplished web designer, you will need professional help with your site. However, there is no need to go overboard. Time-consuming animation can be counterproductive, since many people find it annoying. If they cannot *skip intro,* they may give up and go elsewhere. It helps to include third-party endorsements and articles that mention you.

The text is really important. Since this is a personal site, you can adopt an informal style that reflects the way you speak. It will help your personality to come across. Ask someone to check the grammar and spelling. Then show a pilot version to a few people before it goes live. What is their first impression? How do they *feel* about what they see? Make sure your site is easy to navigate, so people keep coming back.

If you have both a personal and a business website, make sure their messages are consistent, with the same look and feel. Stelios' personal website, at *stelios.com*, is particularly striking. It uses the same orange background as the companies trading under the *easy* brands, and provides links to each of them. You can then decide how to set up the links on your site. John's personal website has a link to Purkiss & Company's website, but not the other way round. Clients and candidates generally look at *purkiss-company.com.* People who have read his books often start at *johnpurkiss.com* and then follow the link to *purkiss-company.com.*

Once your site is up and running, it helps if people can find it quickly when they Google you. Your site's ranking will be determined by a number of factors that change from time to time. These include the number of links with other sites. You or your web designer can find out more about this in *Search Engine Optimization for Dummies,* which we have included under Recommended Reading.

If you are employed and appear on a corporate website, make sure it conveys the right message. If possible, check any material that mentions you before it goes live. Try printing out any pages that include your biography or photograph. The result may be very different from what you see on the screen. The photos can come out in many different sizes. Is your photo up to date and accurate? If you have aged 15 years or dyed your hair a different colour, it could cause embarrassment when you meet people face to face.

Here are some examples of personal websites:

www.davidralphsimpson.com	Artist
www.karymullis.com	Biochemist
www.kathrynpinker.com	Cartoonist
www.neilmullarkey.com	Comedian
www.stelios.com	Entrepreneur
www.maxthurlow.com	Journalist
www.simonlaffin.com	Non-executive director
www.hawking.org.uk	Physicist
www.mitraalicetham.com	Pianist
www.sting.com	Singer/songwriter

Blogs

Blog is short for *weblog* – effectively an online diary. As well as passing on information and opinions, *bloggers* post pictures, videos and audio recordings. New blogs are created every day and the *blogosphere* is growing fast. A blog extends your Web presence and can help you communicate with people. If they set up alerts on their computers, they can read any material you add right away.

Before you start a blog, it is worth deciding what you want to say, as well as how you want to say it. Blogs are essentially personal. The challenge is to remain authentic while keeping people's interest. A good reason for starting one is to share ideas and experiences that you believe may be useful to others. A blog enables you to update people on what you are thinking and doing. You can also use it to get their feedback on your work.

Newspapers and magazines
One of the quickest ways to become visible on the Web is to be quoted in the press. Articles can remain visible for years. If you become an expert in your field, journalists will approach you at some point. It is worth adding those who write about you and your work to the contact list we discussed in Chapter 10. They may be interested in further material. If you are a reliable and accurate source, some will keep coming back. Journalists work to tight deadlines, so they rely on key contacts for an opinion or a quotation that helps to build their story. Many local newspapers and specialist magazines have a small staff and are short of interesting copy. You may find that they publish your article or press release verbatim. However, if you attempt to force-feed a story to journalists, particularly on the national press, it can backfire. It is much better to treat them with respect and build a reputation as a reliable source of information.

It is best to avoid giving opinions on other people or contentious situations. Quite apart from the legal risks, negative remarks reflect badly on you, the commentator. If an article says you "declined to comment", it still helps to build your brand. The fact that you were mentioned shows you are an authority. Declining to comment helps to build your reputation for discretion and professionalism.

Television and radio
The audiences for both these media have become highly fragmented. Before spending time on a television or radio appearance it is worth checking how many people tune in and what their backgrounds are. If you are being interviewed, it is essential to be well-informed and confident. You should also check why you are being

interviewed and the context in which it will be broadcast. When David Royston-Lee was Head of Career Management Services at KPMG, he was interviewed for national radio on the subject of time management. A few days later he and his colleagues gathered to listen to the broadcast. You can imagine David's horror when the lady interviewed before him explained that she saved time by not wearing any underwear. Another man on the programme said he brushed his teeth while going to the toilet.

Seize opportunities to speak to people in groups
One of the best ways to reach more people is to speak to them in groups. It could be two or three colleagues or clients. It might be ten people around a table or hundreds at a large venue. You could appear on television or on a webcast. Whenever you stand up and say something useful to a large audience, good things happen. Someone might want to discuss a job or consulting project with you, or invite you to speak at another venue. Being a speaker gives you credibility on which you can build.

You may be afraid of public speaking. Many people are terrified. They worry about what the audience will think or say about them. Some people in the audience are also afraid – afraid that you will talk for hours, make weak jokes or endlessly promote your business.

You can overcome this, first by changing what you focus on. Unless you are a professional entertainer, you have probably been invited to speak because you know something that could help the audience. All you have to do is *focus* on helping them. It is rather like the mindfulness meditation we discussed in Chapter 14. If you focus on one thing, it shifts your attention away from everything else, including any unhelpful thoughts. Instead of being self-conscious, you will literally forget yourself. Once people realise you are making a sincere effort to help them, they usually relax and pay attention. Even if you are talking about your own experiences, you can focus on how these will help your audience. Most of them will want to learn from your talk, rather than dismissing it as an ego trip.

You can also visualise a successful outcome, in the way we described in Chapter 14. For example, you can visualise people enjoying your talk, getting involved and asking questions – as well as applauding enthusiastically at the end.

Beyond this, public speaking is a question of preparation and practice. The more thoroughly you prepare and the more often you speak, the better you will become.

Get to know your audience and ask them to help you
You may already know your audience well. If not, there are ways to break down barriers and build rapport. One is to find out about them before you speak. Talk to the organiser a few days beforehand. Ask about the audience's backgrounds, what they want from your talk, what they like and do not like. Their nationalities and cultural backgrounds are also important. If you are going to speak to them in a language other than their mother tongue, think of ways to make it easier for them.

If you arrive at the venue early, you can chat with members of the audience. Those who get there first are usually keen to hear what you have to say. If you talk to them and find out their names, you will already have a few supporters when you stand up and speak. They are likely to ask good questions and contribute to the discussion at the end of your talk.

Moving around helps you connect with your audience. Some speakers appear rooted to the spot, twisting their neck so they can read words off the screen behind them. It is better to walk out from behind the desk or lectern and engage with your audience, looking at the screen now and then. If you are talking to a small group, or have a radio microphone, you can walk among them, which is even better. Some talk show hosts do this to great effect.

Speak to one person at a time

If you are speaking to a large audience, you may find yourself staring into space, particularly if you are dazzled by floodlights and your eyes have not adjusted. It helps to focus on one sympathetic person at a time and talk to them. To begin with, you may have to focus on someone you can barely see. They and the people around them will usually pay more attention, because they feel involved. Once you have spoken to them for a few seconds, pick another person in a different part of the room. That way, different groups will be drawn in. Make sure you include someone in the back row and someone on either side of you, so everyone feels involved.

Some television presenters use a simple technique. Although millions of people may be watching, they think of one friend or family member. Then they look into the lens and talk to him or her. It helps the presenter to remain relaxed and confident.

Apply the Minto Pyramid Principle

Your talk will be much easier to deliver if you structure it carefully. Then you can relax, put your message across and answer questions. Listeners will grasp your argument and remember more of what you have said. You can do all of this using the *pyramid principle* developed by Barbara Minto.*

At the top of the pyramid, your presentation should convey the main message. For example, "Building your brand will transform your career". This message can be broken down into a series of statements, the first of which is "You already have a brand". This becomes the heading on the first slide. You can then break this statement down into a series of points – usually between two and four. If you use Microsoft PowerPoint, it will help you to apply the pyramid principle. When we give talks on *Brand You,* our first slide often looks like this:

You already have a brand

o "Your brand is what people say about you when you are not in the room." – Jeff Bezos, Founder of Amazon

o It's not just who you know, it's who knows you.

o Most people do not manage their brands. You can.

You can help to keep the audience focused on what you are saying if you convert a slide such as the one above into four slides. The first shows just the title. The second shows the title and the first bullet point. The third shows the title and the first and second bullet points. The fourth shows the title and all three bullet points.

---

* This technique is explained in full in *The Minto Pyramid Principle: Logic in Writing, Thinking and Problem Solving*. See Recommended Reading.

Some people memorise a speech to accompany their slides. This is a daunting task and usually makes them sound wooden. Equally, you should avoid reading the text word for word, which is boring and causes 'death by PowerPoint'. It is better to use the slides as prompts, so you *talk about* one point at a time. You can add examples and anecdotes as they occur to you. If you have met some members of your audience, you can include examples that are relevant to them. You will then speak naturally, as you would during a conversation. If possible, allow people to ask brief questions as you go along. They will pay closer attention and learn more. If you relax and enjoy it, your audience will feel good about you and your message.

Humour breaks down barriers and keeps people interested. Some speakers tell set-piece jokes, but that has its risks. People may have heard the joke before. They may not share your sense of humour, particularly if they are from a different culture. For us it feels more natural to make light-hearted remarks as we go along. It is certainly less risky. In some countries such as Britain there is a tradition of self-deprecating humour – making remarks at your own expense. Elsewhere this is not common practice. However, you can still have fun. Your audience would prefer to be entertained as well as informed.

An ideal format is a presentation consisting of 10 slides, each of which communicates one point, supported by a series of sub-points. If you allow 2–3 minutes per slide, 10 pages of PowerPoint will give you a presentation lasting 20–30 minutes. That leaves plenty of time for questions and/or exercises. Twenty to 30 minutes is as long as many people can concentrate without a break. They will be grateful if you keep it brief.

Consider writing a letter, an article or a book

If you enjoy writing and are good at it, an article for a newspaper or magazine can help to build your profile. Writing a letter to the editor is even easier, especially if you do so by e-mail. It is best to say something constructive which other readers will find interesting, rather than simply attacking another person's point of view.

Writing a book requires a lot of effort, but can work wonders for your brand. To begin with, it will strengthen your existing relationships. If anyone has read your book, they are very likely to think of you next time they have a need. Books can also have a big impact on people you have never met. Most people keep books longer than other material and/or pass them on to friends and colleagues. If your book is published commercially by a third party, it helps to confirm that you are an expert.

Identify the market and the competition

If you are an expert in your field, you may wish to write a 'how to' book. If so, it is best to address a specific problem. This will help to make it a *must-have* for your readers, rather than a *nice-to-have*. A good example is *Getting To Yes,* the classic text on negotiation that has sold over two million copies in 20 languages.

It is worth visiting a large bookshop to get an idea of what has already been written on the subject. The shop assistant may know of any best-sellers. You can also ask potential readers if they have read anything similar. Did they like it? Would they recommend it to a friend? Once you find a book on the subject you have in mind, look carefully at the style of writing and any case studies that are included.

Some books are written only for the UK or the US market. You can increase your sales by adopting an international approach. One example is *The Tao of Coaching,* by Max Landsberg, a former Partner with McKinsey who is now a Partner with Heidrick & Struggles. His book has sold over 150,000 copies in 20 languages. It is a good idea to write for a global readership. You should also test your manuscript on some non-native speakers of the language in which you are writing. The clearer your text, the easier it will be to translate.

You can still sell a lot of copies in one market, if your book meets a pressing need. A former colleague of ours, Semi Cho, wrote *Global Talent – How to Overcome Cultural Barriers and Become a Globally Competitive Professional,* in Korean. The population of South Korea is 58 million – a little less than France or the UK. Nevertheless, her book appeals strongly to many Koreans' desire to work in international corporations, or see their children do so. It sold 60,000 copies in its first six months and became a top-ten bestseller. Despite living in London, Semi has become well-known in South Korea and now speaks at conferences throughout Asia.

You may spot a gap in the market while you are looking for a book to recommend to other people. John Purkiss and Barbara Edlmair could not find anything to help the hundreds of candidates who contacted them in search of a job. They therefore decided to write *How to be Headhunted,* which was published in 2005.

Once you see an opportunity, you can estimate how big it is. How many people are potential purchasers and how badly do they need the book? Then you can choose a title that will appeal to them. You may change the title between now and publication, but having a *working title* gives you a sense of direction. You can check each idea for a title on Amazon, to see whether anyone has used it before in the same subject category.

Publishers want to know about the competition your book will face. However, it may actually *help* you if other writers have established a readership for your subject. If you have something new to say, people will buy your book too. You can get an idea of how well other books are selling by looking on amazon.com and amazon.co.uk. There are also Amazon websites for the French, German and Japanese markets. The rankings are updated hourly. If you are already in discussions with a publisher, they are likely to consult Nielsen BookScan. It will show them how well similar titles have been selling in the UK, Ireland, Australia, South Africa, Italy, the USA, Spain and New Zealand.

Publishers look for credible authors. They want manuscripts that are *authentic* – written by people who know their subject first-hand and are experts in their field. There is much to be said for writing with a co-author. If you have similar values and expectations, you can produce a much better book than either of you would on your own. There will also be two of you to promote it once it is published. Our experience with *Brand You* is that 2 + 2 = 8 (at least).

Make your book entertaining as well as informative

It is easy to write a turgid book on a subject you know well. It is harder, but a lot more fun, to write a book that brings your subject alive and makes it accessible to a wide readership. A good technique is to imagine you are going to read it aloud, with no visual aids. Listeners will want to understand it straight away, with no footnotes or further explanation. Otherwise they will switch off. This approach also makes it easier to turn your manuscript into an audio book, tapping into another large and growing market.

If you base your book on material you have used to teach people, you will already know what they find most useful, most difficult and so on. You will still need to experiment to ensure that readers enjoy the final version and recommend it to others. We do this by giving drafts to friends from different backgrounds, and of various nationalities. The book evolves from one draft to the next.

Consider other types of book

If you are already well known, an autobiography or a book based on your experience and opinions can work extremely well. The best-seller lists in some countries contain lots of them. Politicians, generals, sportspeople and broadcasters have all written best-sellers in this genre – or have had them written for them. They have strong personal brands already, so publishers and readers flock to them. Even convicted criminals have succeeded.

Your book does not have to be about you at all. It could be about a relative, as in the case of *Ken Purkiss – 50 Photos*. Although John and his friends produced it to raise money for charity, it proved unexpectedly popular among his business contacts. Since photography involves capturing the moment, often in unexpected ways, it fits well with the Magician, John's preferred archetype. Books such as this can strengthen your brand by illustrating your heritage in the way we described in Chapter 11. It is rather like the Jack Daniel's adverts that talk about the company's founder and its tradition of whiskey-making in Lynchburg, Tennessee. See *jackdaniels.com*.

History and biography work well for politicians. Winston Churchill is known for his four-volume *History of the English-Speaking Peoples*. William Hague has written books on Pitt the Younger and William Wilberforce. Writing about your forebears emphasises your heritage and strengthens your brand.

17

Becoming Famous

A large following can bring you many opportunities. People in music, sport and the cinema have achieved international fame and used it to extend their brands into new markets. A much larger number have done this on a national scale. Alan Sugar built up Amstrad, a consumer electronics company in the UK. He has since chaired Tottenham Hotspur Football Club and become a major property investor. He is also the star of *The Apprentice* on BBC TV, a role played by Donald Trump in the USA. Some people are rarely seen in the national media, but are well-known internationally in their sector. Dr Barry Cohen is an American plastic surgeon who has written books, launched his own range of skin-care products and opened a chain of clinics on both sides of the Atlantic. See *bjcohen.com* and *beyondmedispa.com.*

Famous face or famous name?

What kind of fame would help *you* or hold you back? Some people are recognised wherever they go. This may help if you are a model, an actor or a television personality. At the very least you will get a better table in restaurants. Singers such as Sting and Bono have used their fame to lobby for environmental causes or social change.

However, fame can have its disadvantages – most obviously the loss of freedom. You may have to pay extra on planes and in hotels, just to keep away from the general public. You may need a bodyguard to go shopping or attend a social event. Relationships become more complicated if people want to be seen with you.

Another option is to have a famous name without a well-known face. Johannes Vermeer, one of the best-known painters of the Dutch Golden Age, only painted himself from behind. We have little idea of what he looked like. Doris Lessing is a Nobel Prize-winning novelist, but few people would recognise her in the street.

It helps to have a famous relative, particularly if they evoke the same archetype as you. Stella McCartney's career as a fashion designer has benefited from Paul McCartney's brand. He also evokes the Creator in his song-writing. Roger Bannister is known as the first man to run a mile in under four minutes, thereby evoking the Hero. His son Clive has pursued a career in finance, most recently as a senior executive with HSBC. His father's Heroic achievement is usually mentioned whenever Clive is interviewed in the press. It is part of his heritage and helps to strengthen his brand.

Do you want to be a celebrity?

The dictionary definition of celebrity is being famous in your lifetime. However, it has also come to mean being famous for being famous. Celebrity status is fine if you have built your brand on your talents and values. It will give you extra momentum in pursuit of your purpose. Al Gore's political career has provided a launch pad for his campaign to combat global warming. As he says in his speeches, "My name's Al Gore. I used to be the next President of the United States."

Many celebrities become famous without discovering a particular talent or identifying their purpose. They evoke the Ordinary Guy or Girl and people feel they are "just like us". They charge lower fees than talented celebrities, helping to make reality television highly profitable. Unfortunately, thousands of others can do the same. It is hard to build a long-term career on this basis.

Staying famous can require effort, but even traumatic events may help, provided you evoke your archetype consistently. Some successful actors and singers evoke the Outlaw. They break the rules, even at the expense of their health. If they spend time in rehab at The Priory or the Betty Ford Clinic, it helps to sustain their fans' interest in them. Although these establishments charge a lot for medical treatment, the publicity is exceptionally good value. Once the media latch onto a story about drugs or alcohol, it reaches millions of people. We are not suggesting you do the same. However, you may find other creative ways to evoke your archetype.

It is sometimes said that all publicity is good publicity. We disagree. Publicity is only good if it fits your purpose. A famous example is Gerald Ratner, the former Chief Executive of the Ratners jewellery chain, which he built up from 130 stores to 2500 over a period of 10 years. In 1991 he told a conference that a sherry decanter sold by his company was "total crap". His remark wiped £500m off the company's value, which swung from a large profit to a large loss. That remark also cost him his job.

As the chief executive of a public company, it might have been better for him to evoke the Ruler. Another helpful archetype would have been the Ordinary Guy/Girl, since Ratners made gold jewellery accessible to people on moderate incomes. By denigrating his company's products he evoked the Outlaw, with destructive consequences for both the company and his career. He has since made a comeback with *geraldonline.com*, a large online jewellery business.

How famous do you want to be?
Being famous will help you when you attend a meeting or social event, or appear in the media. People will feel they *know* you. However, you must also be *authentic* – true to your values and your purpose. Then there will be no surprises as you build new relationships.

Few names or faces are recognised worldwide, and most of us do not need that level of recognition. It is better to define the group you want to reach and become famous among *them*. Who do you *want* to recognise you? It could be a few thousand people in your country. It could be those who work in your sector, in several countries. Once you have defined your target audience, you can think about how to reach them. Ideally you should use several media at once. As we mentioned in Chapter 1, when people have heard about you in three different ways, you begin to stand out in their minds.

18

Protecting and Extending Your Brand

Although your brand is an *intangible* asset, it could easily become more valuable than any *physical* asset you possess. It is therefore worth protecting.

Manage your brand name(s)

The steps you take to protect your personal brand name will partly depend on how famous you are or intend to become. If you decide to be visible on the Web, it is best to register your domain name both as a .com and using your local suffix. For example: *johnpurkiss.com* and *johnpurkiss.co.uk*. This can be hard if your name is a common one. You can check whether your name is available by visiting a site such as *freeparking.com*. It is easier if you have an unusual nickname. For example, Gordon Sumner became known as Sting because he wore a black-and-yellow striped jumper that made him look like a wasp. See *sting.com.* You may even be able to register your name and logo as a trademark.

Treat people fairly

Every undertaking involves risk. In the theatre, the cinema and early-stage investing, some new ventures always flop. However, you can ensure that everyone involved knows the risks they are taking and is treated fairly. You can also make sure, before you take on a project, that you have the time and resources required to do an excellent job. If you have to cancel the whole thing, or close down a business, you can do so ethically and transparently.

Some people damage their brands without thinking about it. They gain in the short term but lose in the long term. If you behave impeccably, you will keep attracting people and new opportunities. You will be much better off overall.

Take the initiative – deal with problems straight away
If your colleagues share your values, you should have few problems. However, if they do anything that could damage your brand, you may have to distance yourself. Turning a blind eye is a big risk. It may be enough to tell them how uncomfortable you feel about what is going on. The advantage of saying how you *feel* is that no one can contradict you. Neither have you judged them or accused them of anything.

If they are doing something illegal, it is worth consulting a lawyer. You may wish to resign or terminate your relationship. The longer you allow things to continue, the greater the potential damage to your brand. The business world and politics offer many examples of reputations and entire careers blighted by scandal. If it emerges that you acted swiftly when you found out what was going on, it may even *enhance* your brand.

You can extend your brand in ways that confirm your brand identity
Brands are not single products or services. As we said in Chapter 2, a brand is a symbol that guarantees a particular experience. Brands give meaning to life and can take

many forms. They can be extended to new products and services, provided the *essence* of the brand is maintained. Kodak started out selling Box Brownie cameras, but has since moved on to selling photocopiers. As Andy Milligan points out, "Once people experience a brand and like it, it acquires the legitimacy to offer them something else: maybe a different kind of product, but one with similarities in form or function or emotional resonance."

Successful corporate brands have done this for many years. Virgin started as a record company. The brand has since been extended to air travel, financial services, mobile phones and many other products and services. The Easy brand has been extended from easyJet to easyCruise and beyond. Brands can be extended if they make a strong promise to customers, including a consistent purpose and set of values. When the Virgin Group launches a new product or business, customers expect innovation, value for money and fun. If a brand keeps its promise, it becomes more valuable than before. Broken promises will damage it.

The same applies to *your* brand. If you are thinking of doing something new, ask yourself if it will fit your purpose and your values. Will it evoke the same archetype as before? Leonardo da Vinci consistently evoked the Creator, whether he was painting portraits or designing flying machines. A modern example of the Creator is Philip Hughes, the co-founder of Logica, the IT services company. He became known as a painter while he was still Chairman. Since leaving the company he has pursued a full-time career as an artist.

Imagine your brand is a tall building with a large atrium. When visitors enter at street level, they immediately get a feel for its purpose. It might be a department store selling everything for the home. There are counters and shop assistants everywhere. When visitors look up, they see balconies on the floors above. Your department store can add any product range that is consistent with your purpose and your values.

It is best to extend your brand to areas where you are credible or can become so quickly. David Royston-Lee has applied his background as a psychologist to both marketing and public relations. John Purkiss has used his knowledge of executive search and personal development to write books that help people in their careers.

EXERCISE P: Extending Your Brand

Write down – in as much detail as you can – everything you enjoy doing and do well. Include the things you do at work and in your spare time. What are the underlying talents? What are the values that make those activities meaningful for you? Write down all the other talents you have discovered in yourself and enjoy using, but are *not* using right now.

Now make a list of new activities you would like to try. Could you begin any of them now? Experimenting with and extending your brand helps you maintain a high level of energy. It keeps you at the forefront of what interests you most.

David Beckham: a case study in brand extension
David Beckham is a good example of how to build a global brand and extend it beyond the original activity. The material in this case study is taken from Andy Milligan's book, *Brand It Like Beckham – the Story of How Brand Beckham was Built*. If you are interested in personal branding and/or football, we highly recommend it.

Beckham has a strong element of the Magician. He may not be the greatest footballer the world has ever seen, but he is exceptionally skilful, often transforming his team's fortunes. He also evokes the Ordinary Guy consistently. This strengthens his appeal to people who feel that he is 'just like me'. He has built a unique brand that is admired around the world by men and women, young and old.

Beckham has benefited from major changes in his market. These include the rise of the English Premier League to international prominence, fuelled by revenues from terrestrial and satellite broadcasting. FIFA's decision to promote the game globally has greatly extended his international reach. The tournaments in the USA in 1994 and Korea/Japan in 2002 helped to build an international market.

Many people turn their noses up at David Beckham. However, his critics will not be attracted to him anyway if the Ordinary Guy archetype does not appeal to them. The key to his success in building a global brand is that he has evoked the Magician and the Ordinary Guy consistently. This has enabled him to extend his brand across several product categories.

Here are some of the steps that have worked well for Beckham in building his personal brand:

- At the age of 16 he appointed an agent to look after his affairs. This enabled him to concentrate on improving his game.

- He signed with Manchester United, which has a tradition of stylish football and now has more fans in Asia than it does in the UK and Ireland.

- He has cultivated the brand values of dedication, style and down-to-earth honesty. They come across in everything he does, from his determination to be the best footballer he can, to the way he follows fashion and expresses his emotions openly.

- He is softly spoken and appears humble. This increases his appeal in Asian cultures that are founded on respect.

- His lack of fluency in his mother tongue is consistent with the Ordinary Guy and has made people warm to him. When asked by a journalist if he was learning Japanese in time for the 2002 World Cup, he replied, "I'm still tryin' English."

- His good looks have enabled him to extend his brand from football to fashion. In 2001 he launched the Police eyewear collection in the UK. This was the first campaign that did not draw on his image as a footballer, but promoted his looks and fashion sense instead.

- His marriage to former Spice Girl Victoria Adams gave him access to the world of entertainment and the tabloid press. She also took his surname, helping to spread the Beckham brand to a wider audience.

- He consistently pursues excellence, both on and off the field. Becoming England captain in 2000 brought him no direct commercial benefit, but the emotion and imagery surrounding the England brand, with its three-lion logo, have undoubtedly strengthened his own.

- In 2003 he moved from Manchester United to Real Madrid. His new club had an even greater heritage, reputation for style and record of achievement. At the time it was the most successful club in Europe.

- He provided Real Madrid with a ready-made marketing channel into Asia, where he is widely revered. This was reflected in his contract, which included key clauses relating to image rights. The move also gave him access to the Hispanic market, with over 425 million native Spanish-speakers worldwide. Both he and Real Madrid were sponsored by Adidas, which made him more valuable to them.

- He and Victoria appointed the pop impresario Simon Fuller, who had launched the Spice Girls, to build the Beckham brand globally.

- In 2007 Beckham announced his decision to join LA Galaxy in Los Angeles. Having built a strong presence in the Spanish-speaking market during his time with Real Madrid, he was now well placed to develop his brand in the USA. Hispanics represent around 15% of the US population and have a keener interest in soccer than their non-Hispanic compatriots.

- Beckham had long dreamt of setting up a football academy, which has now become a reality. See *www.thedavidbeckhamacademy.com*. It supports one of his aims, which is to help young people develop their football skills.

Be selective about endorsements and recommendations

If you are well known, you may have opportunities to endorse products and services. If you choose them carefully, they can strengthen your brand as well as generating extra revenue. However, they must fit your brand image. Some Hollywood stars have appeared in advertisements for mundane products such as furniture that bear no relation to their brand and have thereby damaged it. By contrast, Nicole Kidman can only have enhanced her brand by appearing in the world's most expensive advert – for Chanel No. 5. This mini-film, directed by Baz Luhrmann, lasted nearly three minutes. Viewers commented afterwards that she looked like the most beautiful woman in the world.

People in all walks of life make endorsements, sometimes without considering the effect on their brands. If a recruitment consultant asks you to suggest candidates, be wary of recommending a friend with a poor track record who is always looking for a new job. The recruiter may conclude that your judgement is also poor. It is better to help your friends directly than to misrepresent their abilities to others. Many recruitment consultants have a drop-down menu on their database so they can mark you down as a good or bad source. If they think you are good, you will be one of the first people they call about an exciting opportunity.

19

Co-branding

Co-branding is when two or more brands join forces to bring a product or service to market. If their strengths complement each other, the end result will be much more powerful than anything they could have achieved on their own. They are sometimes described as *brand buddies*. One example is the highly successful *Nike+*. Runners' shoes tell them via their iPod about their pace, the distance covered and the number of calories burned. The iPod also provides downloads of suitable running songs.

Co-branding can also involve *personal* brands. Here are some examples:

- David Beckham joining Real Madrid, as described in the last chapter
- Daniel Barenboim conducting any major orchestra
- Oprah Winfrey interviewing other celebrities.

Co-branding also occurs when you work on a project with someone or join a company. Before you do so, it is worth considering the effect their brand will have on yours. You can take references. You can also talk to a few people informally without disclosing your plans. Everyone has their admirers and detractors, but common themes emerge quickly. If you are considering joining a company, you can track down people who used to work there and get their feedback. At least you will be going in with your eyes open. Do you feel comfortable being associated with them? How will it affect your brand? What are their values, as demonstrated by their behaviour? We are not suggesting you only work with people who have the same talents or skills as you. It is usually better if those are different from your own. However, we *do* recommend working with people who have similar values. You are likely to agree on most things and spend far less time on management issues. You will also enjoy it and be more successful.

Think carefully before you add to your CV/résumé

Every move you make affects your brand, whether you are choosing a business school, joining a company or starting a new one. Some people are so cautious that they never take a risk. Their CV lists one blue-chip name after another. However, the biggest successes often occur when this pattern is broken and someone goes beyond what is expected of them. For example, many successful entrepreneurs start their businesses just after being fired.

One solution is to start off in a blue-chip organisation and take risks later. The techniques and disciplines you learn at the outset will serve you well throughout your career. Your pedigree will give people the confidence to invest their time, their reputation and/or their money in you. If you start a business that crashes and you have to get a job, you will still be a strong candidate. Many employers prefer someone who is highly qualified but has also shown a willingness to take a calculated risk.

Piggy-back on other people's brands

You can build your brand faster if your customers have strong brands that reflect well on you. *Consumer* brands are particularly good. People often think that the companies in question are much bigger than they really are.

Purkiss & Company's first assignment was to recruit a Finance Director for Fitness First – Europe's leading health-club chain. Although its revenues at the time were 'only' £100 million, it had a market capitalisation of £500 million and was a member of the FTSE Mid-250 index. It was well known among people living and working in large cities. Fitness First is now the world's second-largest health-club chain, with over a million members. Its brand really helped to launch Purkiss & Company.

20

Building a Team

As we mentioned in Chapter 1, hierarchies are in decline. Organisations are becoming flatter and flexible teams are more and more prevalent.

Archetypes are very useful for building teams. Understanding your own archetype makes you more aware of those that other people evoke in their work. You can then choose colleagues who fit with you and the market you serve.

John and his colleagues were once asked to recruit a finance director for a large company that owns hundreds of pubs and is quoted on the London Stock Exchange. After visiting several pubs and meeting the board and management committee, John concluded that the organisation evoked the Ordinary Guy. The beer and food were of good quality but also very affordable. The head office was open-plan and everyone ate in the same canteen. There was a minimum of hierarchy and they addressed each other by their first names.

The shortlist consisted of eight candidates, all of whom evoked the Ruler to a greater or lesser extent. They were all qualified accountants and had been finance director of a large division or an entire company. The board of directors wanted an element of the Ruler, to help keep hundreds of pubs under control and steadily expand the business.

Candidate A evoked *only* the Ruler. He had spent most of his career working at the head office of large companies. The board liked his financial control experience but felt he lacked any personal connection with their business.

Candidate B evoked both the Ruler and the Hero. He had been captain of the school rugby team and had nearly become an officer in the Royal Marines. Having trained as an accountant, he had specialised in tackling difficult projects and turning around failing companies. However, the board did not want the Hero. Their business had grown successfully over many years and they did not feel it needed rescuing.

The successful candidate evoked both the Ruler and the Ordinary Guy. He had attended an undistinguished school in a small industrial city. He had been one of very few pupils who had gone to university. He enjoyed spending time in pubs and the board felt he would fit their culture.

You can use archetypes to build *your* team. It may be that you and your colleagues evoke an archetype that reflects the underlying business. However, each member of the team can also evoke another archetype that reflects their particular role.

One example is an early-stage software company that evokes the Ruler. It helps companies to control their finances and manage risks. The chief executive is a former professional climber who does everything in a disciplined way. This evokes the Ruler and appeals to customers who wish to rule their business empire. He has a similar appeal among investors, who know that he is taking good care of their money. However, he also evokes the Magician, having bought the software from a liquidator in order to turn it into a viable business. The sales manager has a similarly disciplined approach. However, he also evokes the Ordinary Guy as he contacts potential customers and builds rapport with their staff at all levels.

Archetypes are a useful complement to other models
You may be familiar with other psychological tools such as *Myers-Briggs,* which, like the archetypes described in this book, is based on the work of Carl Jung. The Myers-Briggs model measures personality styles on four dimensions that Jung described in his book *Psychological Types,* published in 1920. In 1962, Isabel Myers and Kathryn Briggs published a questionnaire for identifying different kinds of personality: *The Myers-Briggs Type Indicator.* They used Jung's model, which they relabelled as follows:

- E = Expressive   or I = Reserved
- S = Observant   or N = Introspective
- T = Tough-minded or F = Friendly
- J = Scheduling   or P = Probing

If you take a Myers-Briggs test, it will measure you on each of these four axes. This can help to predict who will get along with whom. For example, someone who has a strong F orientation will find it easier to get along with a fellow F than with a strong T. You can also make sure there is a suitable balance of personalities in a team. For example, a strong P will tend to examine data continually, feeling more comfortable *before* a decision is made than when it *has* been made. By contrast, a strong J will want to get the job done, and will feel more comfortable when a decision has been taken and implemented. In order to strike a balance between analysis and decisiveness, you need both types of personality in a team.

How do archetypes fit with Myers-Briggs? The short answer is: with difficulty, even though many people have tried to make them fit. A more practical approach is to use each for a different purpose. It is like shining a light on an object from different directions. Each reveals a different facet of the person.

EXERCISE Q: Other People's Archetypes
Write down the names of people you work with closely. Which archetypes do they evoke consistently? If each evokes a different archetype, do they complement each other and make the team stronger? Do several of you evoke the same archetype? If so, would your team be stronger if it included people who evoked other archetypes?

Conclusion

The best way to market yourself is to build your personal brand. However, you have to know what you are selling. In other words, you have to know yourself. For most of us, this is a lifelong voyage of discovery.

We hope you have found the exercises helpful. If you have skipped any, we strongly encourage you to go back and fill in the gaps. Discovering yourself is the most powerful way to learn. We have provided a framework to help you do so.

Here is a checklist to make sure you have completed the key steps:

- Identify your talents
- Identify your values
- Identify your unique combination of skills and experience
- Keep your purpose in mind
- Decide which archetype (or two) you are going to evoke consistently
- Make sure your work fits your purpose
- Create your contact list
- Offer to help people whose work you admire
- Summarise what you do in three seconds
- Make sure that what you say and do evokes your main archetype

- Focus on serving people rather than trying to get something from them
- Remain in the present. Accept things as they are
- Mentally rehearse your desired outcome
- Work out the ZOPA before you negotiate your remuneration
- Become more visible, using the appropriate technology
- Protect your brand and consider extending it
- If you can, piggy-back on other people's brands
- Use archetypes to build a strong team around you.

If you complete each of these steps you will build a strong brand identity and be memorable. The effects are frequently dramatic. We look forward to hearing your story.

We wish you every success!

John Purkiss & David Royston-Lee

Websites:	*www.johnpurkiss.com*
	www.davidroystonlee.com
Twitter:	*www.twitter.com/JohnPurkiss*
	www.twitter.com/davidroystonlee
Facebook:	*www.facebook.com/JohnPurkiss*
	www.facebook.com/davidroystonlee

Recommended Reading

It's Not How Good You Are, It's How Good You Want To Be, by Paul Arden (Phaidon Press, 2003)

Raving Fans: A Revolutionary Approach to Customer Service, by Ken Blanchard and Sheldon Bowles (HarperCollins Business,1998)

The Crystal-Barkley Guide To Taking Charge Of Your Career, by Nella Barkley and Eric Sandburg (Workman Publishing, 1996)

Wholeness and the Implicate Order, by David Bohm (Routledge Classics, 2002)

Flow – The Classic Work on How to Achieve Happiness, by Mihaly Csikszentmihalyi (Rider & Co, revised edition 2002)

Getting To Yes: Negotiating Agreement Without Giving In, by Roger Fisher, William Ury and Bruce Patton (Random House Business Books, revised second edition 2003)

Search Engine Optimization for Dummies, by Peter Kent (John Wiley & Sons, third edition 2008)

Warren Buffett Speaks – Wit and Wisdom from the World's Greatest Investor, by Janet Lowe (John Wiley & Sons, second edition 2007)

The Hero and the Outlaw – Building Extraordinary Brands through the Power of Archetypes, by Margaret Mark and Carol S. Pearson (McGraw-Hill Professional 2001)

Follow Your Heart: Finding Purpose in Your Life and Work, by Andrew Matthews (Seashell Books 1997)

The Writer's Journey – From Inspiration to Publication, by Julia McCutchen (Firefly Media, 2004)

Brand it Like Beckham –The Story of How Brand Beckham was Built, by Andy Milligan (Cyan Books, 2004)

The Minto Pyramid Principle: Logic in Writing, Thinking and Problem Solving, by Barbara Minto (1996 edition, available from www.barbaraminto.com)

Ogilvy on Advertising, by David Ogilvy (Prion Books, new edition 2007)

Managing Your Self: Management by Detached Involvement, by Jagdish Parikh (WileyBlackwell, new edition 1993)

How to be Headhunted, by John Purkiss & Barbara Edlmair (HowTo Books 2005)

Are You Ready To Succeed? – An Unconventional Guide to Personal Transformation in Work and in Life, by Srikumar Rao (Rider & Co 2006)

Madonna – the Complete Guide to Her Music, by Rikky Rooksby (Omnibus Press, second revised edition 2004)

How to Become an Icon, by Simon Silvester, Executive Planning Director, Young & Rubicam:
http://emea.yr.com/icon.pdf

Archetypes

For your convenience, here is a summary of the archetypes:

The Caregiver	Helps and protects from harm
The Creator	Compelled to create and innovate
The Explorer	Explores and discovers
The Hero	Acts courageously to put things right
The Innocent	Seeks purity, goodness and happiness
The Jester	Has a good time but may convey a serious message
The Lover	Finds and gives love and sensual pleasure
The Magician	Transforms situations
The Ordinary Guy/ Girl	OK as he or she is. Connects with others
The Outlaw	Rebels and breaks the rules
The Ruler	Takes control. Creates order out of chaos
The Sage	Helps people to understand their world

We plan to publish a sequel to *Brand You* in 2010. If you would like to be notified when it is available, please go to *www.brandyou.info* and register online.